RESILIENT IN BUSINESS

The Founder's Roadmap to Lead Through Uncertainty
and Win the Long-Term Game

Jad Atwe

Copyright © 2026 BY JAD ATWE

Published by Business Optimization Partners LLC

Austin, Texas

Resilient in Business / Jad Atwe —1st ed.

ISBN 979-8-9943411-0-0 (pbk)

ISBN 979-8-9943411-1-7 (eBook)

Library of Congress Control Number: 2025927819

www.resilientinbusiness.com

To God — the power that gives and takes
and the wisdom behind both

PRAISE

"Jad Atwe's Resilient in Business meets founders where certainty disappears and leadership becomes personal, in other words when inevitable chaos hits hardest. Having worked with leaders across industries, I know how isolating it can feel when everything shifts and challenges arise. Jad's honest and substantial writing draws on real experience, shaped by early lessons in entrepreneurship and by building a successful business in a new country. His storytelling immerses readers in the lived experience of leading through uncertainty, while his ROOTS method provides a solid foundation for growth and success. Resilient in Business is a trusted companion for entrepreneurs who want to lead with clarity, resilience, and intention in the face of complex strategic decisions and ambiguity."

Dr. Douglas Scherer
Speaker and Bestselling Author

"Navigating uncertainty is the norm for any leader but doing so without a grounded internal state leads to reactive decision-making and exhaustion. *Resilient in Business* provides a clear roadmap for regaining control amidst the noise. Jad Atwe demonstrates that by upgrading our internal capacity to process stress, we unlock the clarity and focus required to win the long game. A vital resource for the conscious leader."

R. Michael Anderson MBA MA,
Author of Leadership Mindset 2.0

"Resilient in Business serves as a paramount book for businesspeople who find themselves in survival mode. This text offers a superior alternative to the adopting attitude of struggle, overwhelm, and pushing through at all costs in business. The book delivers immense value by shifting the focus from external business tactics to business leaders' internal personal operating system, as the growth of companies. Some key topics in this insightful book include the significance of resilience in business, the importance of effective emotional regulation under pressure, and performance as a reflection of how leaders operate internally. Ultimately, this book provides a practical roadmap that helps businesspeople shift from a reactive attitude to a more resilient perspective."

Professor Bruno Roque Cignacco, PhD
Author of the book "The Art of Compassionate Business"

"This book is refreshingly raw, honest, and informative. Through personal stories of growth, struggle, and rebuilding, Jad Atwe takes you on a true rising-from-the-ashes journey of entrepreneurship. He then introduces the ROOTS system, thoughtfully bridging the physical and neurobiological into a practical personal operating system that naturally scales into business. The tone is inviting, direct, and easy to digest—no fluff, no wasted words. It's an ode to self-growth, discipline, and self-care, grounded in real-world scenarios that make the lessons highly relatable and immediately applicable. I highly recommend this book for anyone looking to strengthen their life, business, and health with clarity and intention."

Andreh Custantin
Owner of Maha Design Studio

"Working with Jad Atwe over the past six months has been an absolute game-changer for my business. His expertise in organizational improvement, system-building, and creating efficient procedures is unparalleled. Thanks to his guidance, I am now in full flow, transforming my company with well-structured streamlined processes, and the support of smart tools.

Jad's approach is both down-to-earth and direct, with the perfect balance of humility and confidence. He's not afraid to confront challenges head-on, and his insights are consistently valuable and actionable. His ability to break down complex problems and offer practical solutions has provided clarity and focus at every step of the journey.

If you're looking for a business coach who truly understands how to drive sustainable organizational change, I wholeheartedly recommend Jad Atwe. He is an invaluable partner in achieving long-term success."

Henk Overbeek
Owner of Aidos Accounting

"Entrepreneurship demands more than effort—it demands personal evolution. *Resilient in Business* speaks to the reality that discipline and routine may take years before showing results, but when they do, the compounding effect can be extraordinary. This is a book for founders serious about becoming their best self."

David C Barnett
Small Business Author and Speaker

CONTENTS

RESILIENT IN BUSINESS

PART ONE

AWAKENING AND RADICAL OWNERSHIP

A NOTE TO THE READER

This book is for you, the founder, the builder, the legacy creator, the courageous one who dares to dream big, execute, and turn their vision into reality. It's for those who know deep down that they were made for more, but who feel like the current way of running their business isn't sustainable.

If you've ever caught yourself thinking, *I know I'm on the right path ... I just can't keep doing it this way*, then this book is for you. More specifically, it's for:

- The visionary who's tired of holding everything together, and who feels their goals are out of reach

- The ambitious founder who keeps showing up, even though they feel like they're running on fumes and are on the verge of burnout

- The leader who's grown their business, but feels emotionally flat, as though the joy is gone

Building a business is a significant undertaking: you're taking care of fires and pressure from all directions while managing and motivating people to help pull you towards your goals *all while* trying to stay connected to your values and show up as your best self. But most conversations around entrepreneurship don't talk about the emotional cost of leading a business and managing all the juggling you need to do. We hear that perseverance is a must and with this book I'm pleased to offer you a roadmap to how that can be possible, especially when you're dealing with chaos day in and day out.

You might be here because you're:

- **In survival mode, or on the verge of burnout.** You wake up tired. You're doing the right things but feel disconnected from your energy and motivation.

- **On a rollercoaster of emotional highs and lows.** One good week feels amazing, the next sends you spiraling into doubt, fear, and panic.

- **Trying to push past a revenue ceiling.** You're trying different tactics, working hard to move your business forward, but it feels like you are running on a hamster wheel, and having a hard time reaching better results.

- **Struggling to step away from your business.** Even when you're "off," your mind keeps looping through everything that needs to be fixed or done.

- **Going through a stressful time.** You're navigating a tough situation and aiming to figure your way out of it.

- **Constantly putting out fires.** You're moving from one problem to the next, without space to zoom out, lead from your vision, and actually focus on what will move your business forward.

- **Guilty when you take breaks.** The to-do list never ends. There's always something more to do, and rest feels undeserved.

- **Detached from what you really want.** You're meeting goals and making progress, but your business no longer feels aligned or fulfilling.

- **Overwhelmed by decision fatigue.** Your focus is scattered. You're drained, and every little thing feels urgent and heavier than it should.

- **Doing it all alone.** You don't have the kind of support that truly holds space for you as a business owner—emotionally, mentally, or strategically.

- **Hard on yourself.** You push through setbacks without really processing them or celebrating the milestones. There's no real system for recovering—only surviving.

- **Unclear on what "resilience" actually looks like in business leadership and you are confusing it with pushing through at all cost.** You've built the business without considering the internal structure essential to supporting you so you can play the long-term game.

If any of this sounds familiar, you're definitely not alone. There is a different way to build—a way that allows you to set yourself up for success, that supports you in being effective at leading the ship without costing you your well-being or your sanity or sabotaging your results. This book will walk you through it.

How to Read This Book

This book is not meant to be read once and then forgotten. It provides a roadmap to be lived daily as it supports you in shifting from being somewhat (or highly) reactive to becoming deeply rooted in practices that help you lead effectively, build your support infrastructure, and increase your entrepreneurial resilience. This book is meant to meet you where you are. My recommendation is to give yourself space and read at your own pace. Pause to reflect and highlight what hits. Most importantly, come back to yourself and consider how the teaching applies to you; then identify areas you need to work on most.

This book provides a proven framework that is transformative; however, the shift only happens when you slow down, reflect, and actually implement the recommended practices daily. Ultimately, you have agency; follow what resonates with you. *Resilient in Business* is simply a resource you can return to when you are ready to build capacity and lead your business from alignment. With that being said, let's get started!

INTRODUCTION

Why Resilience Matters, and
Why You Must Play to Win

This book is for the founder who has a lot on their plate. Who is stressed from juggling way too many priorities yet passionate about their entrepreneurial path and determined to build something meaningful—to "make it." In the pages of this book, I will dive deep into entrepreneurial resilience, the most important factor of your business's success, and provide a road map for your Resilient in Business Operating System™ or Resilient in Business OS™. This is the personal operating system that supports you, the founder, in shifting from stressed, reactive, and overwhelmed—working hard without actually moving forward—to building the structure and rhythm, and adopting the practices, that support you in leading effectively, even amidst all the pressure, uncertainty, and chaos of running a business.

Entrepreneurship is a sacred calling not many choose to pursue. You might have chosen this path for one of many reasons. Perhaps you're a visionary who identified a gap in the market; maybe you've overcome a personal struggle and feel called to help others navigate that same challenge; possibly you're a free spirit seeking time or financial freedom; maybe as a result of life circumstances you might have found yourself directed on this path without prior planning. Whatever your motives were, this journey requires a great deal of courage. In addition to the day-to-day stress that comes with existing on this planet, you decided to assume another dimension of anxiety: the pressure that comes with being a business owner. In a world that teaches us complying is the norm, that only teaches how to be a good contributor to the system, being brave to pursue this path—to stand up for your future, for your family, to seek freedom, to find your own path, *and live life on your terms*—is a rebellious act. So, congratulations, you are to be celebrated, as this journey is not for the faint of heart!

Running your own business is deeply fulfilling and comes with tremendous rewards. But here's the truth: no amount of preparation can fully equip you for what lies ahead. Some variables are in your control, but many are not. No strategy can fully make your business immune to challenges. It doesn't matter how much experience you've accumulated, how much training you have undertaken, or the fact that you've earned a business degree. It doesn't even matter how tough you think you are: the journey will still find a way to humble you. Challenges are an inevitable part of the game; it is difficult to totally predict or plan for everything that might go wrong. It's safe to say that reaching a breakthrough in business comes down to two main components: entrepreneurial resilience— building capacity and being equipped with systems and practices that support you in persevering and staying the course despite the chaos and uncertainty—and luck, which typically shows up *after* you've been doing the right things for a period of time.

Stepping into this journey, you might have expected some challenges and decided that, when the time comes, you would figure it all out along the way. And you're right! That's a good approach. But have you wondered how bad the situation might get? How far are you willing to go to drive your business to success? What's your tolerance level for the effects this journey might have on your life, relationships, and finances, or your physical and mental health?

At this point, you might be wondering *who is this guy and why should I even listen to him?* A very valid question. So, here is a little bit of a background to make my case. I've always had a big vision of living an entrepreneurial life and, for as long as I can remember, I've been excited about the future and all that I want to accomplish. I started my career as a civil engineer, in which I pursued both a bachelor's and a master's degree. Passionate about construction, the first business I started was a general contracting firm that also did real estate development.

Advocating for and writing a book about entrepreneurial resilience never made it to the vision board until recently. But the idea to write *Resilient in Business* came during one of those difficult times when I was handling more challenges than I thought possible. I can confidently say I am naturally a very optimistic and creative problem solver. I believe there is always a way to get out of a tough situation. Yet, out of the blue, I found myself up to my elbows in problems with no solutions in sight: I had no idea what to do next and could see no way out of my predicament. After exploiting all options, I was exhausted on all levels. I remember sitting in bed one night at my lowest point, new to journaling but still wanting to make sense of it all. The magnitude of my situation was so ridiculous that I thought it is important to document. I found myself rambling on for fifteen pages. It's wild how we don't realize how much we carry until we pause and put it all into words.

Each individual challenge was manageable on its own. But when they all came at once, everything felt very heavy. I was beyond my limit emotionally, mentally, and financially. My bank accounts where empty, my credit cards and lines of credit were all maxed out, more debt was accumulating every day, and there was no clear way forward.

Amidst all the chaos, what surprised me most was how I had not reached a total breakdown. How was I still standing? The truth is, this wasn't my first difficult season; however, what had previously felt like "rock bottom" was nothing compared to this. This was the *actual* rock bottom.

Despite all the chaos, one thing remained very clear: I wasn't giving up on my entrepreneurial journey. It is my soul's calling, all that I am excited about, my path. To me, the freedom in all its forms, the personal growth and evolution that comes from going through the hoops, and the creativity of designing and delivering your services in a way that provides value to your clients and addresses a need, are all extremely very fulfilling. My vision was (and is!) big, and I was just getting started.

This book isn't about my story, though I'll share parts of it in the upcoming chapter to illustrate how a series of unexpected events can push you off the rails. What I've learned along the way is that challenging times force us to go through a major personal transformation where we must let go of our old self—of our ego. This process humbles us, and takes us back to the basics, to identifying what actually matters.

As a founder, there is a lot to coordinate if you want to ensure you are running a successful business. Some of the problems are under your control; others are beyond it. And even though you might not necessarily be navigating severe challenges that pull your business off course, you might find yourself at times stuck in a pattern where, despite all your hard work, it feels like the business is not getting the success you are hoping for.

What you might not realize as the founder of a small business is that your business is a reflection of you. You are the one with the authority to set the vision, rhythm, tone, standard, and direction. In a small environment, where you are the sole director and everyone else is there to support you, the biggest barriers to success become internal.

They are tied to and influenced by your personal performance, the structure you set, and the systems and personal beliefs you operate by ... and they are less the result of external circumstances. Business performance tends to be a direct mirror of how you personally operate, even if you are leading a team of employees.

When you see the same patterns keep repeating—like jumping from one strategy to the next and not being able to break through a certain revenue ceiling, or when you stay in a loop of attracting the same type of clients that are not best suited for your business, or when despite all efforts your team does not seem to be reliable or able to produce consistent results— the repeating patterns are a sign your business's problems are not what you think. The system in which you personally operate is the root cause of the bottlenecks, although you might not realize it. The way you show up and lead yourself and your business makes the difference between being able to navigate confidently or folding to the chaos and calling it a day.

We see examples of this repeatedly in how a change in CEO at a firm affects the leadership and the team and, in turn, the results a business produces. Another example is when two businesses working in the same industry and subject to the same circumstances end up with dramatically different results: one appears to be thriving while the other is barely getting by. Here is where stepping back and examining how your personal operating system is serving you is essential in getting to the root cause of the unfavourable patterns and setting yourself up for success.

At this point you might be thinking *why the emphasis on resilience, and what the hell is a personal operating system?!* One of the most widely cited definitions of resilience research is from Luthar, Cicchetti, & Becker[1] which states: "resilience refers to a dynamic process encompassing positive adaptation within the context of significant adversity." In simpler terms, resilience is the ability to face

---

[1] S.S. Luthar, D. Cicchetti, and B. Becker, "The construct of resilience: a critical evaluation and guidelines for future work," *Child Development* Volume 71, No. 3, (May 2000: 543).

and navigate adversity, unfortunate events, and challenging times while remaining grounded, and bouncing back or regaining your state of stability.

For some founders, a certain event will knock them down and nudge them out of business, leaving them terrified, scarred for life, and giving up on their vision. For others, that same event is nothing more than a valuable lesson they walk past and then carry on to build a legacy. The question that presents itself here is: *What makes for this difference?*

Research shows that our resilience is revealed in how we respond to negative external events. Research also shows that our ability to be resilient isn't a personal trait we are born with, and we don't have a fixed amount of it. Instead, it's a capacity that expands as we adopt the right practices, strengthen our mindset, and learn to meet challenges with greater skill.

As a founder, navigating uncertainty on a daily basis is normal. Being resilient in business isn't just about bouncing back from a difficult circumstance or overcoming setbacks. It is critical to embody entrepreneurial resilience on a daily basis, to build the capacity for rising above uncertainty, staying grounded, clear, and focused, and executing at a high level. It's about positioning your business for success despite the exterior noise, without burning out—or calling it a day.

In the small business world, your business's results are a direct reflection of you, the sole director. Your business evolution cannot outpace your capacity to lead it. A few examples of this are the following: you can't scale when you don't have the capacity to respond to the demand, you can't make the right decisions when you are drained and exhausted and have no energy, you can't take the right actions when you have false beliefs that are not serving your expansion, you can't run your business effectively when you haven't set the right support infrastructure in place. In order to mitigate the root cause of what keeps the business stagnant, you have to start by looking at and upgrading how you personally operate. When you realize how much of the business results are a direct outcome of how you operate and not just external circumstances, you can see that business reliability and resilience come downstream to founder resilience. Founder resilience is a result of implementing a personal operating system that includes practices, tools, and rhythm to support you in building your capacity to lead, being effective at managing uncertainty and being able to successfully steer the ship to that next phase of success.

That's the objective of the Resilient in Business OS™. It's a five-step roadmap that addresses the root cause—the blind spots that might be holding your business back—and allows you to increase your entrepreneurial resilience capacity, successfully lead through daily uncertainty, and win the long-term game.

I am a forever student, always seeking knowledge about everything that helps move my business forward. Going through difficult times made me more determined to figure out what it actually takes to effectively lead a business. My curiosity, coupled with my ADHD, took me on a path I had not anticipated: being certified in business coaching, executive coaching, and business systemization, and learning about the science of resilience, positive psychology, neuroscience, mindset, behaviour change, and best entrepreneurial practices. Turns out I had been unconsciously leaning on the five practices that are detailed in the Resilient in Business OS™, to remain grounded, focused, and motivated so I could keep pushing forward despite the madness in my life.

The reality is that motivation or hustle alone are a guaranteed path to exhaustion and burnout. The old saying "it is important to work smarter not harder" very much applies to founders, more than anyone else. Going through a rough patch does not mean we are not meant for this, or that we should call it a day. All we need is perspective and a commitment to following the structure, systems, rhythm, and practices that will carry us through uncertainty and allow us to take our businesses to its next level of success.

This book isn't about hustling harder or pretending to have it all figured out. It is about being grounded with the personal operating system that serves your business's success.

Life is too short for mediocrity, too precious to spend on the sidelines, and far too valuable to waste running in circles without progress. All of those paths come at a cost, and it's higher than you might realize. The entrepreneurial path can be filled with many challenges. If you are brave enough to take it on, you might as well play to win, and fully live your life on your terms.

Ultimately, you're the only one who can define your story. So, the real question is: What would you like it to say? Are you ready to ditch the struggle and hustle and build your aligned legacy?

The intention of this book is to leave you better than it found you. To outline the roadmap to the Resilient in Business OS™ — the personal operating system that will support you in leading your business effectively.

Throughout this book, you'll find reflective questions at the end of most chapters. The purpose is not to reflect for the sake of reflecting, but to inspire action where necessary. Results are only achieved when we move beyond knowing and into implementation. This is how we work with founders and CEOs as they position themselves and their companies for the next stage of growth.

As a thank you for picking up this book, I've put together a free on-demand workshop at www.resilientinbusiness.com/resources. It's a guided experience designed to help you pause, reflect, and explore how the ideas in this book reveal insights about your current reality as a founder or CEO. I recommend going through it after completing the book to deepen your understanding and contextualize the concepts to your own journey.

Before I sign off, if this book has resonated, connect with me on LinkedIn and send me a message. I would love to hear your story and how this project helped you.

CHAPTER 1
HERE'S WHAT HAPPENED

Hitting the Wall and Awakening to Purpose

The entrepreneurial journey is often described as a roller coaster ride. Some days you feel motivated and on a high, others feel like you're hitting the jackpot, and there can be moments when you feel like the ground beneath you is shaking. You're doing everything you can to hold on, but the pressure doesn't let up. You feel like you're running out of air as you attempt to satisfy all the demands of running a business.

Reflecting on those low points through my own experience, is what inspired developing The Resilient in Business OS™ that I'll be walking you through in this book. The practices you will find here became essential in maintaining my sanity, navigating a minefield of challenges, and setting up my business for success; I am confident that it will have a key part in your journey, too. So, here's what happened ...

I grew up in Lebanon, a beautiful country in the heart of the Middle East that due to its geographic location has been unstable, since the dawn of time. Tuning in to the news channels every evening feels like watching a new episode of an action movie that never ends. Because of the nature of the political scene, business success in Lebanon often required being part of "the system," which I had no interest in.

I always knew I wanted to be an entrepreneur, especially in construction and real estate development. That dream has lived in me for as long as I can remember. My father was a general contractor, architect, and developer, which gave me a front-row seat to the ups and downs of business over the years.

Being very good at math and physics, and passionate about the construction industry, I earned a bachelor's degree in civil engineering. After graduation, I worked as a civil engineer for a year, then moved to Canada to pursue my master's degree in civil engineering as well. One of the major cultural shocks for me at the time occurred during a discussion with a local friend. He was rambling on about his plans for the next five years and then asked what were mine. A very fair question, which at the time was a new concept for me. Projecting this far into the future had never crossed my mind, as the place I came from is very unpredictable. Major events can occur and conditions can change dramatically between breakfast and lunchtime, which, in hindsight I realize makes one accustomed to living one day at a time, being spontaneous, and figuring things out as you go! Never mind *five* years—projecting *one* year into the future with any certainty is just not possible. Needless to say, that conversation was one of the realizations that led to the beginning of my immigration journey.

After my master's, I spent three years in Toronto working for engineering firms, long enough to secure permanent residency, a milestone after which registering a business becomes easy.

As soon as that came through, I felt like a free man. It was finally time to pursue my entrepreneurial dream! I handed in my resignation and registered my general contracting and custom home-building firm the next day. I was excited and optimistic about the future.

The journey started with major renovations, full-gut projects, home additions, and speculative new builds for subdivision-style homes. As with any new business, the beginning was turbulent. It doesn't matter how long you've been in an industry or how much you think you know, there's a big difference between being in the passenger seat and being in the driver's seat.

After being in business for a few years, and gaining a deeper understanding of the market, I realized that positioning the business in the luxury custom home space would be the most financially rewarding. Especially in a space where residential general contracting is seen as a commodity, where anyone with a truck can call themselves a contractor, and many homeowners are influenced by home renovation shows that create unrealistic expectations.

At the time, Toronto's real estate market was booming, driven by low post-pandemic interest rates, increased immigration, low housing supply, and limited land for development in the area. During the three months between December 2021 and February 2022, land prices in my market jumped by about 23%. My plan was to establish a name in the luxury market by building and selling on a speculative basis first, as this approach would help create a track record in that market and provide an example of the great quality of work I provided. At the time, the numbers looked promising, too good to ignore.

So, in February 2022, I purchased two lots in a premium area, one on my own and another with a joint venture partner. At that point, optimism in the industry was at an all-time high. The sentiment from all experts was the same: the conditions would keep the market immune from any corrections. There was a significant shortage in available inventory, the demand outpaced the supply, and the prices would remain high and continue rising, until further notice.

Little did I know that this was the peak of the market. The government decided to interfere in an effort to help with affordability, so they banned foreign buyers from purchasing real estate, a useless move that didn't move the needle. And due to soaring inflation, the Bank of Canada started a series of gradual interest rate hikes over a couple of months, a move that disrupted the market and sent prices on a downward spiral.

By the time we completed the design and municipal permit approval process, and started construction, the project financials didn't look as promising anymore. New builds couldn't compete with existing market inventory due to the escalated cost of construction.

I hadn't started construction on one of the lots purchased, so instead of building new, it made more sense to pivot. I renovated the old existing home on that lot and put the property back on the market to salvage what was left with the least loss possible. The sale dragged on, drained a lot of cash, and ended up creating a significant financial loss.

As for the joint venture project, the existing property was not salvageable; construction was underway and the only viable option was to move forward with it, aim to break even, and retrieve the investment out of it. The market continued to decline and there was a lot of uncertainty around job security, interest rates, and trade issues across the border. This completely froze the market and led to another financial nightmare.

Lending terms for development projects depend on many variables. The lower property values, market volatility, and increased interest rates resulted in the lender not fully financing the required construction loan amount—a very important step that hadn't been an issue prior to this market volatility. So, this meant we had to inject more capital into the project, pay significantly higher fees servicing debt, and find a lender with better terms.

A Terrible Experience
I hired a mortgage broker I had known for years, a "leader" in the real estate investing community. Working with that broker ended up being a terrible experience. He kept lying, couldn't deliver, dragged his feet for months, and made a lot of false promises.

A quick note on money and business partnerships here: going through tough times makes you realize the significance of choosing your business partners wisely. Just because a person wants to be in business and work with you, does not mean they will make a good partner. Before entering into any business partnership, think hard. Do you really know who you are working with? Are your values and visions aligned? And do you both have the same tolerance for stress and pressure? Will you still be aligned if things don't go as planned?

During all the chaos, I can see many instances where my relationship with my joint venture partner could have gone sour and become a major source of stress. Yet, it was a stroke of luck that the person I had partnered with on that project was aligned with me on everything; we rolled with the punches together in sync and we figured it all out one storm after another. We're both pragmatic and have a high tolerance for stress and risk, so it worked out okay.

I know many people who are amazing as friends; however, a business partnership with them would not be a wise decision. Vet potential joint venture partners thoroughly. Just because someone can fund the project and is eager does not mean they are the right person for the task.

In my general contracting business, meanwhile, that year was the worst. Four different client projects canceled as rising prices and market turbulence led people to hold back from starting. The previous year, I had invested heavily in marketing, the highest budget I had ever allocated, yet the work that was intended to come from it was all cancelled. That meant incoming cash had completely dried up and I was left with nothing but expenses.

As we reached 70% completion of the build project, the high cost of running expenses led to the inevitable: running out of capital to finish construction. All my funds were either tied up in the project or in personal property that was not liquid. So, we had to raise money to get the project over with and move on, to close the chapter. That ended up being no easy task. Before the market turbulence, more than thirty investors had been ready and excited about partnering. But the market shift had either put most of them in a tough spot—having to deal with their own cash flow issues—or led some to move to the sidelines.

That's when the tough questions started kicking in. How do we move forward from here? What can I let go of temporarily? And what truly matters right now?

I decided to put the home I was living in on the market. The funds from that sale would help us complete the build and get out of the project. More than two years later, my home was still listed, waiting for the right family.

Between personal and business mortgages and other expenses, I was bleeding a lot of cash. The amount is too embarrassing to admit. Payments were due every two weeks. Navigating that stretch felt like living on the edge every day, scrambling. I would make one mortgage installment and ask for an extension on the next, for months. The mortgage officer was not impressed. We ended up raising the remaining funds from four different sources and completed the construction.

Aside from the financial constraints, I had hired a friend to represent the sale of the three properties. For the record, that's a terrible criterion for choosing a real estate agent, as much as you would like to support a friend's business. The process turned into a disaster. The agent had their own set of personal issues, and communication and execution were a mess.

Back in Lebanon, things weren't any better. Lebanon had gone into another war with Israel and my parents were right in the middle of it. The damages were severe, all over the country, and there was no end in sight for the misery that was unfolding.

All of the above happened simultaneously. I found myself trying to manage my team in the middle of financial loss with debilitating cash flow issues while managing key vendors who turned out to be incompetent, to say the least, all while navigating an uncertain market without a way to predict the outcome, *and* dealing with the emotional stress of knowing beloved family members were in a life-threatening situation, literally under fire.

Typically, navigating any one or two of those situations is manageable: eventually you just master the art of tiptoeing around them and figuring a way out; but with everything happening all at once I felt like I was jumping from one major fire to the next. Sleep was not an option. As I mentioned earlier, although I've always been a creative problem-solver, I was maxed out financially, mentally, and emotionally. My youngest sister was living with me at the time; as ridiculous as this sounds, if it wasn't for her financial support, I have no idea how I would have made it.

When everything around you is falling apart, there's only one place left to go: inward. Being in the chaos leads you to go back to questioning everything in a way that you wouldn't have otherwise done, even when things are modestly working out. *How can I get out of this? What story am I writing here? What do I actually want from this life? What is serving me and what is not? Is this path getting me closer to my vision? Or is it time to pivot and work differently? How should I move forward?*

Technically, we're the ones who got ourselves into this, and we're the only ones who can get ourselves out. That's where the next chapter begins: awakening to the truth that it's all about you.

CHAPTER 2
AWAKEN TO THE TRUTH:
IT'S ALL ABOUT YOU

Take Radical Ownership of Your Life and Destiny

The beauty of running a small business is that results your business produces tend to act like a mirror held up to your face. You are responsible for what's working and what isn't. So, congratulations—both your actions and inaction have brought you here.

One of my long-time friends owns a design firm with about five employees. She became one of my first business coaching clients early on. She's an excellent salesperson. Their lead flow was strong, signing clients wasn't an issue, and people were genuinely excited to work with her firm. The problem was service delivery. The quality of the work delivered was inconsistent, timelines were missed, and commitments to their clients were regularly overextended.

It was clear they needed structure: documented workflows, and systems that supported consistent reliable outcomes. We mapped the systems and processes, clarified what it actually takes to complete a job successfully, and determined how to set clear client expectations. Everyone on the team was on board, and no one had any questions or concerns.

When I checked in three months later, I wasn't surprised to learn that nothing had changed. The business was still operating in the same chaos. "My team doesn't like structure," she told me. In my head I was thinking "well, who the hell is in charge over there?" But I wasn't surprised because knowing my client, I could tell she doesn't like structure herself. And she did not yet fully appreciate the freedom she would get from ensuring the team did not reinvent the wheel every single time a new client came in.

Addiction to chaos is a real thing. In this case, responding to fires made her feel busy and important. "Saving the day" provided a boost to the ego, reinforcing the belief that her presence and input were necessary for things to move forward in the right direction. When that is taken away, she feels like she is no longer in control. The problem wasn't the team, but the lack of clear intention and follow-through. The team was there to support and was waiting for the cue.

This is a typical example of how stagnation occurs. The problem here was systems and processes, in other cases it could be something else. The founder was not fully ready on a subconscious level to take the steps necessary to build capacity and position the business for the next level, so she unintentionally sabotaged her business's growth.

There tend to be conflicting opinions around the term "self-made," even when it applies to founders who have experienced a level of success. Some say that since we can't build something meaningful in isolation—that since leverage and support are necessary—then this title can't be claimed; no one is fully "self-made".

Running a business is an ever-evolving game. Every season comes with its particular set of challenges to navigate. As you scale, and move up from one stage to the next, the nature of your challenges and their complexity evolve, but they still remain. You can always bet on the fact that uncertainty exists in one shape or another. The reality is that you have free will. Whatever your motives were to pursue and stay on this path, you're the one who has decided to step into the arena and continue to face this pressure, day after day, despite the uncertainty. That part is all you.

As the owner of a small business, casting the vision and embodying the courage to play this game can't be outsourced. You are ultimately responsible for making sure your business is set up for success. You need to work diligently to navigate muddy waters; no one will do it for you. Your actions and how you respond to external circumstances will either yield growth, stagnation, or survival. That's how running a small business is all about you.

As a small business owner, people are not drawn to request your services or be part of your team because of the brand identity, website, or logo. All of those bells and whistles are necessary, but not the reason why you're in business. You're in business because you created a system people trust.

If you have already been moderately successful, the good news is that, yes, you *are* self-made: you kept showing up when quitting or doing nothing would've been easier.

Just like many aspects of life (relationships, health, life path, etc.) there are no guarantees. A relationship you once were passionate about might experience turbulence, fade away, take a turn you didn't expect, or turn out to be a total mismatch.

Running a business is similar. It can surprise you and take turns you may not have anticipated. No matter how well you plan, how diligently you work, or how strategic your decisions are, there will always be unexpected variables that can be outside your control: the market shifts, people change, new technology emerges, tariffs are imposed, and a pandemic explodes out of nowhere—and those are just a few examples of the unpredictable bumps that might arise along your road. With limited exceptions, it is highly unlikely you will be fully shielded from uncertainty while in business. It's not a matter of *whether* you will be tested, but *when*.

When chaos hits, it's easy to start pointing fingers to blame the economy, your competitors, or the people who didn't support you. And, sure, those things might all play a role. But they're usually not the reason we stay stuck. Just as business success is all about you, more often than not the root cause of many problems—and the real battle— is internal.

It takes courage to step back, zoom out, try to make sense of what is going on beyond the surface level problem, and face the truth; and, yes, it's uncomfortable. But that's where true change and breakthroughs become possible.

Being at the level you are at, the journey can feel lonely. You're the one who has to make sense of what's really going on, the one to make the hard calls where high stakes are involved. You're the one who must manage a tricky situation without full knowledge of all the variables involved and without any warranties on the consequences of any of your decisions.

You might not currently be surrounded by people who truly get what you're going through. The weight you're carrying might not be fully visible to anyone else. And, in some cases, people might be aware of your challenges but are not equipped to provide meaningful input. The sooner you realize this fact the easier life becomes.

The reality is that this is your path and your calling, and it's no one else's business. Not everyone will understand what you're building, and most won't be cheering you on. You're navigating territory many can't comprehend, and that's okay. They don't have to understand, and you don't need approval or public buy-in to walk your path. Not everyone is meant to walk through that season with you.

Protecting Your Energy

That means you have to be your own advocate. Protecting your energy is a must. So is being intentional about who gets access to your inner circle. It means letting go of what no longer serves your growth—whether it's people, outdated habits, limiting beliefs, or comfort zones that have become cages keeping you from evolving to your next stage of business success. Refusing to let go of what doesn't serve as you're breaking free will at best slow you down and, at worst, make it downright impossible.

Success in your new chapter will require a new version of you, a new identity. One that evolves, even when the process is uncomfortable. You don't need someone else to believe in you. Most people are still struggling to believe in themselves. Their doubts are usually projections of their own fear, not reflections of your potential. When someone questions you, it's not always personal. But if you internalize it, you start carrying limitations that were never yours to begin with.

Going back to the basics means that if someone is not qualified to help you figure out a certain issue, and their life is not affected by your work, then their thoughts, opinions, and limitations are irrelevant, whether they are called friends, family, or anyone else. They definitely do not have any voting rights with regard to what is happening, what you intend to do, or where you intend to be in your life.

Challenging times are uncomfortable and painful to experience, but within this unfortunate process is where you find the quiet confidence that comes from realizing that you are capable of jumping through hoops and taming fires you haven't anticipated. With the right practices, you can master the art of scoring small wins and building unshakeable conviction in your path and your ability to "make it." Those moments help cement your inner authority and your successful founder identity.

Filtering out the external distractions and having the courage and conviction to trust your own voice above all is critical, even when you might be feeling alone. Your intuition holds the right answers—answers you can't hear until you become ruthless about trusting yourself and filtering out everything that is not serving you, filtering out all the noise. This is your life and your legacy, after all, and you are responsible for steering the ship in the right direction.

If you've been given a vision and purpose—by given I mean felt drawn to it—and you've resonated mentally and emotionally with it, then this pull is not random. You were called to walk this path for a reason. You owe it to yourself and to your family to remain resilient and see it through.

Sure, it's a bumpy road, a "rollercoaster ride," some would say, a journey that may come with unfortunate events. The cost can sometimes feel heavy and might be perceived as a setback. When things move slowly, and not as anticipated, it might feel like you are out of breath and paddling upstream; but when you accept that turbulence is just part of the game, you start meeting challenges with a new kind of strength.

So, yes, you are self-made because you kept showing up and took ownership when it would've been easier to walk away. You made the hard decisions no one else could make for you.

At this point we have established that:

- Being in the arena is a reflection of your courage

- It is all about you

- It is your responsibility to take control and steer the ship along the right path

- Resilience is the key to playing the long-term game, and

- A robust personal operating system is critical to being able to handle what is coming and lead effectively.

You might be thinking, *well that all sounds great, but how?*

Great Question. In the next chapter, I'll introduce you to the Resilient in Business OS™, the structure, systems, and practices that allow you to navigate uncertainty with calm and unshakable confidence. It will ultimately set the foundation that positions you and your business for success. So, if you are ready, let's get started!

PART TWO

THE RESILIENT IN BUSINESS OPERATING SYSTEM™

CHAPTER 3
INTRODUCTION TO THE
ROOTS FRAMEWORK

The System That Builds Structure,
Sustainable Rhythm, and Momentum

You've probably heard the mainstream motivational advice claiming that all it takes to succeed is to outwork everyone else. That if we work harder, hustle more, put in more hours, and stay positive, eventually we will be successful. But what if that's not what's missing? What if the real issue isn't that you have a flawed strategy or you either aren't motivated enough or aren't working hard enough? What if the root of the problem is how we're leading ourselves and our businesses, and how we're trying to hold it all together on the inside?

Over the years, I have seen many examples of great businesses—some I hired directly on my build projects—that delivered a great product and were in high demand but that just a few years later were closed by the owner.

It is deeply saddening to hear the unfortunate news, especially knowing the person behind the business and knowing how hard it is to create demand, build a team, and reach a point of success. In hindsight, the trajectory toward the demise of their businesses was predictable, given how they were leading. Sometimes an owner simply sabotages their business's growth.

In one case, a concrete forming company, the founder's team was great, and so was the quality of the finished product ... when they had a chance to finish it. One person, the founder, managed three crews while doing all the estimating, sales, marketing, operations management, and financial management. He handled the clients, too, all while refusing to hire help in any of these areas due to lack of trust. This man had to be all over the place; he was spread too thin, trying to control everything.

This balancing act ends up being a nightmare. Poor communication with clients, missed deadlines, construction schedules that were not met, suppliers that were not paid on time, certain parts of the work not being completed, and, ultimately, furious clients dogged his every step. In chaos like this, it doesn't take much to lose your sanity or get into trouble. A few angry clients leading to no payment, and issues with the wrong hires, ended up leaving the founder drowning in problems and unable to overcome the madness.

Another example of a failed venture I came across related to a talent acquisition agency. The founder had an MBA and all of the qualifications on paper that scream "this guy is very knowledgeable!" I met with him prior to the pandemic as he was trying to expand his business into Canada and he wanted to hear my take on the market. His business sourced and then connected engineering and architectural talent from overseas with architectural and engineering firms in North America. The difference in hiring costs makes sourcing from abroad attractive. This man had raised money from investors and was attempting to figure out how to make the venture work.

At that point, there was not significant competition in this niche, although since then some people have replicated the model successfully. We met at a coffee shop and had a long chat. Reflecting back on the conversation, it is now clear how limiting beliefs, lack of confidence in execution, and lack of emotional maturity ended up sabotaging this founder's success. His hesitation was obvious. A few years later, the venture no longer exists and this person had transitioned into a business consulting role in one of those widely known consulting firms.

Building an Internal System

If we were to exclude terrible business ideas for a second, as well as flawed business models, I think it's fair to say that most founders don't fail because they lack ambition or vision. They fail because they did not build the right internal systems that allow them to increase their capacity to handle and navigate uncertainty so they could transition their business to its next stage of success.

Imagine yourself as a large oak tree, just for a moment. No matter how tall or strong it looks on the outside, it can't withstand the elements if its roots are shallow. To stand firm and resilient in the face of foul weather, it needs to be deeply grounded in its roots. The same applies to you: it is important to build the capacity that will support you as you rise.

We've all heard the surprising claim that most lottery winners end up losing their money and returning to the financial situation from which they started—if not a worse position—a few years after the win. The struggle to manage sudden wealth is attributed to the fact that they haven't built the habits, systems, or identity required to sustain it. Without those foundations, rapid gains often collapse just as quickly as they arrived.

In business, sustaining success, facing uncertainty, or building your business to its next phase of success is not a function of having a business or MBA degree, although those are beneficial for people who want to stand out and climb the corporate ladder. As the founder of a small business, sustaining success and growing your business depends on your ability to build the capacity that supports your entrepreneurial resilience. It comes from how you lead yourself, how you design your personal operating system, the practices you follow, and the structure and rhythm you set. These all facilitate effective execution and position you for long-term success.

Unless you are intentional about designing your personal operating system to increase your internal capacity to lead, you will face three possible outcomes:

- In the best-case scenario you might stagnate, staying stuck at your current level, as your standard way of working does not facilitate growth,

- You might burn out from the emotional roller coaster, the pressure, and the stress that come from the task of taking care of everything and being constantly in reactive mode, or

- In the worst-case scenario, you call it a day and close shop after experiencing a series of unfortunate events or deciding the outcome is not worth the effort

When chaos hits, pushing harder and relying on discipline and adrenaline might get you through for a while, but that pressure doesn't just magically disappear; it ripples into all areas of your life and business. Over time, without a roadmap to stabilize us internally, the chaos pulls us towards collapse.

Most founders are focused on addressing bottlenecks in their sales, marketing, operations, personnel, or whichever other problem of the day has arisen. And, while some know the importance of streamlining their business and setting systems for each different department in their business, they invariably neglect to build the most important system: the one for managing themselves.

As hands-on operators we get caught up in our day-to-day activities and often don't immediately realize the ripple effect of reactive leadership, of being caught up in firefighting and trying to push through at all costs. The way we show up every day and lead ourselves—our internal system—determines how everything else runs around us. And without that, it's easy to stay busy in the same patterns, to chase urgency, drown in a long to-do list, run on low energy, make wrong decisions, exhaust and confuse the team, become physically and emotionally drained, and constantly pivot without direction.

It is important to clarify at this point the difference between a personal operating system and a business operating system. A personal operating system is the founder's internal playbook: the system that shapes how they lead themselves and their business, regulate emotions, observe patterns, remain clear and grounded, make decisions, manage energy and focus, design their support ecosystem, and respond to uncertainty. A business operating system, meanwhile, defines how the company runs—its structure, roles, and accountability systems, metrics, workflows, processes and the rhythms of its meetings, etc.

Before looking at business frameworks, the most critical step is to implement an effective system that supports *you*, the founder, the CEO, the leader, the captain of this ship.

So, how do you set yourself up to consistently lead at your best while navigating the demands of growth, decision-making, and constant uncertainty *every single day*? Obviously, you implement an effective personal operating system!

That's what the Resilient in Business OS™ is all about: a personal operating system customized for what works for you. It's designed to address key practices essential for leading yourself and your business to long term success. It's how you show up with presence and focus, how you identify and let go of what does not serve you, make aligned decisions, build momentum and move with clarity and conviction towards your goals, execute without burning out or drifting off course, and build the eco-system that supports your business along the way.

At the heart of the Resilient in Business OS™ is the ROOTS Framework. This framework is built around five foundational practices that represent the five roots of entrepreneurial resilience. The acronym stands for REGULATE, OBSERVE, OWN, TEND, and SUPPORT. In the chapters ahead, we'll explore each of these ROOTS in depth. But first, let's take a high-level look at what each component is, and why they all matter.

R: REGULATE

REGULATE is about stabilizing your internal state, calming your nervous system, so you can show up grounded and lead with presence, composure, and discernment, especially when the stakes are high. Beyond stress management, REGULATE is about building the emotional and physiological infrastructure that makes sustainable leadership possible.

Entrepreneurs often operate under pressure. Being in states of reactivity, overwhelm, and burnout are often expected, are considered the norm, and the price of being a business leader.

This state does not serve any good purpose and comes at a steep cost that we do not necessarily realize in the moment. You can't "mindset" your way out of chronic stress. Without first restoring nervous system stability, it is very difficult to remain clear on priorities and make sound decisions.

O: OBSERVE

OBSERVE is about reclaiming your power by identifying and breaking free from the unconscious patterns that are not serving you and are hold your business back.

Caught up in the demands of the day-to-day, most founders lead on autopilot, without realizing how much fear from the unfamiliar reality, their previous conditioning and false beliefs, and unresolved emotion are shaping their choices and sabotaging their success.

Observation helps you see those internal loops clearly—so you can interrupt them. The intention here is to build self-awareness in real time and challenge those limiting beliefs, so you can make better moves and break free from the habits that keep you stuck. This shift transitions you from reacting to responding—from fear-based leadership to conscious decision-making; it allows you to step away from the trap of spinning your wheels without seeing the expected results.

O: OWN

OWN is about embodying your winning identity and building aligned momentum. It is about coming back to yourself, to what is true to you, to what motivates you in persevering on this path. OWN allows you to strengthen your inner authority, get clear on where you are heading, and start building momentum towards those goals.

After regulating your nervous system, and observing the patterns holding you back, embodying your winning identity allows you to gain perspective and take the right aligned action.

T: TEND

TEND is about effectively managing your energy and creating a rhythm that sustains your performance.

Amidst the never-ending to-do lists and fires to put out, you might find yourself reverting to pushing through at all costs and reacting to events as they occur. This hustle without recovery, and without a rhythm that honors your energy, gets you on the fast lane to depletion. It also strands you on the treadmill of reactivity: you work hard without being productive, and end up with no time to actually focus on what truly moves your business forward.

TEND has many benefits. Structure, balance, and predictability in your calendar helps calm the nervous system as you know what to expect, and are not just mindlessly reacting to the external demands as they appear, at the same time you become more productive, lead without burning out, and better integrate your work and life.

S: SUPPORT

SUPPORT is about designing strategic personal, relational, and operational ecosystem that provides leverage and work alongside of you towards building a successful business.

Many founders fall into the self-reliance trap, carrying way too much on their own. This often stems out of habit as this is what they have always done, sometimes it is due to pride in their work, or fear of letting go. The problem here is that without the right support structure, it is difficult to go far, your business becomes less reliable.

All of the five ROOTS dimensions are critical to allow you to lead yourself and your business better, to increase your capacity to deal with uncertainty and strengthen your entrepreneurial resilience.

It is important to follow the components of the ROOTS framework in this specific order, as they build on each other. Implementing an effective personal operating system starts with leading yourself first—by regulating your nervous system in REGULATE and gaining the benefits that come with that practice— and progresses to designing the right support ecosystem in SUPPORT, the step that empowers you to amplify your impact and lean on the much-required leverage you need.

Weaknesses in any of those five key dimensions become blind spots that significantly affect your entrepreneurial resilience. They impact how you show up, the actions you take, how motivated you remain, the momentum you create, and, subsequently, the results your business will experience.

Here's the thing:

- Being dysregulated impacts how we see events. It colours our perspective, which affects our decision-making.

- When we don't identify the loops holding us back, we stay stuck in the same loops, working with no progress.

- When we don't align our identity with our future vision, strengthen our self-authority, and start building aligned momentum we become vulnerable, we do not take the right action, and we do not move with the conviction and perseverance necessary to stay the course when it matters.

- Not managing our energy effectively means working hard but not moving forward. We become exhausted with little to show for it.

- And, finally, without a strategic support ecosystem, our operation does not produce reliable outcomes, and it is more difficult to get out of unfavourable situations when they occur; we all know the famous saying "your network is your net worth"

Becoming rooted in these five practices yields a significant return to the evolution of your business. In the chapters ahead, we'll elaborate on this more and we'll explore each element of the ROOTS Framework in depth: what it means, why it matters, and how it fits into your Resilient in Business OS™. As you read, try to identify the weaknesses in your personal operating system.

This book is intended to lay out the road map for the practices that lead to increasing your entrepreneurial resilience, however, the transformation resides in daily implementation of those practices. In the Resilient in Business OS™ implementation process I use with my clients, we go even deeper, as I guide them in bringing this framework to life through science-backed tools, proven best practices, and customizing the system to their unique circumstances, rhythm, and season of business.[2]

The reality is we all have a personal operating system. Whether how we lead ourselves and our businesses is optimized to help us be successful, is another story.

Prior to implementing the Resilient in Business OS™, the first step I take with my clients is understanding how they are currently operating. Through a structured Personal Operating System Audit, we evaluate your Personal Operating System across the five ROOTS dimensions to uncover blind spots, hidden bottlenecks, and self-sabotage patterns that limit your capacity to scale your business.

The results are visualized using the Entrepreneurial Resilience Wheel, which provides a clear snapshot of your Personal Operating System and reveals the patterns shaping your decisions, behaviors, and outcomes as a founder. To book your POS audit, visit www.resilientinbusiness.com

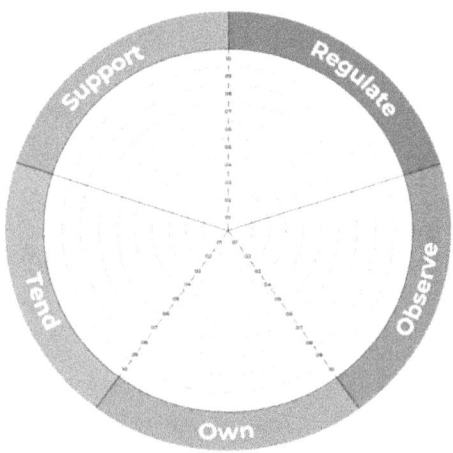

Figure 1. The Entrepreneurial Resilience Wheel, a visualization tool for profiling the strengths and blind spots of a founder's Personal Operating System.

Now the time has come to dive in and talk about the first and most important dimension: REGULATE.

---

[2] To get started with the Resilient in Business OS™ implementation, visit www.resilientinbusiness.com

CHAPTER 4
REGULATE

Master Your Internal State and Lead with Strong Presence, Composure, and Discernment

Amidst the different variables we are managing, it is not out of the ordinary to experience delays, hiccups, bottlenecks, balls dropped, or even a team member's outright negligence. As the person ultimately responsible for the results your business produces, every inconvenience feels personal and can translate into spikes in blood pressure, a constant state of stress and, heck, if it wasn't illegal, you might be very much tempted to get violent at times!

Let's take the construction industry as an example. It's an interesting field where you get exposed to different personalities and competing expectations. In the office, you'll find the professional service types (your engineers, architects, designers) who are amazing people. The suppliers, amazing people as well. However, after the

COVID-19 pandemic, they struggled to commit to anything: prices, delivery, or timelines for a prolonged period of time. On site, you will find the hard-working trades, the people proud of seeing what they physically built come together. And then there are your clients, the party who is excited to get the project over with and enjoy the promised product.

A common scenario I have seen manifest over and over again is when one of those office personalities, or the client, decide to change their mind about the design way too late in the construction process. Those decisions can be very disruptive to the follow of the entire project, and costly in both time and resources. When such decisions are made, they can be sacrosanct, non-negotiable, and ultimately it falls on the trades and site people to make them happen. Depending on the day, what that trade person has already been dealing with, and the amount of re-work required, breaking the news about the new changes can lead to a tense conversation, if not to someone losing it, and at times this can trigger the trade person's own set of irrational demands. Not surprisingly, having the patience of a monk and the skills of a diplomat is important for success.

The nervous system is the bridge between your mind and your body; it's what turns thoughts and emotions into physical sensations. The moment your mind senses a threat, you can feel it in your body. That's because when your brain perceives danger—whether physical, emotional, or psychological—your sympathetic nervous system, the part of the nervous system that prepares you to take action under a threat, takes over. It floods your body with cortisol and adrenaline, your alertness becomes sharper, your heart rate increases, and your muscles tighten. In an instant, your system shifts from feeling safe and present to being in survival mode and wanting to seek protection.

The challenge here is that our brain is wired to protect us, however it can't tell the difference between real and perceived threats. An angry client, a cash flow scare, an unreliable vendor, or a tough conversation with a member of the team all register the same way in our brain as physical danger does. Our heart races, our breathing quickens, and our body braces to fight, flee, or freeze. This protective loop, which we're born with, is designed to keep us alive and away from threats. Apparently, this is what helped us survive the dangerous animals, back in the good old days when we were living together in the wild. However, this amazing feature designed to protect us becomes a trap when we remain in high alert mode, stuck in this endless stress cycle, and we forget to signal to our brain that we are, in fact, physically safe.

When our nervous system is on alert, and we're stuck in a fight-or-flight state, the part of our brain responsible for perspective and reasoning—the prefrontal cortex—goes partially offline. This means that our ability to think clearly diminishes as our focus narrows. Yet this is the default state for many founders, who show up daily with bodies that are chronically tense and with minds that are racing with thoughts of all the firefighting they are caught up in. When chaos becomes the norm, they get stuck in a cycle of responding to urgencies and scanning for the next problem. Eventually, stress and chaos can become an addiction that you unconsciously seek.

You might think this is normal because that's the way it has always been, and you might have convinced yourself this is what being a business owner looks like. The cost of being the boss. Which are all false beliefs. In reality, being stuck in this loop is very taxing on your health, on your energy levels, and on the results your business achieves, as strategic thinking is not possible.

It is common to get in the "no one is going to outwork me" mentality, to get carried away in the main stream entrepreneurship advice of grinding hard, putting in more hours than anyone else, on the way to being the best, beating the competition, etc. There is a time for that, and I am not against being competitive, however, I have also seen this play out poorly over and over again, especially when a founder is in a dysregulated state. In those cases, the harder we push, the more we disconnect from the very qualities that make great leadership possible: composure, perspective, and discernment. We end up trying to lead people, and make high-stakes decisions, while our body is in a constant alarm state. It is easy to imagine how that pans out. Everything starts to feel heavier, slower, and harder than it should; poor judgement ends up being at an all-time high and so does the number of costly decisions.

When our internal system is flooded with stress hormones day after day, our brain loses access to our executive functioning, the part responsible for how we see ahead, relate to others, and make decisions. We start leading from fear rather than foresight. Here is where having some level of self-awareness becomes a great idea.

Regulation of our nervous system restores our capacity to handle difficult situations. When our body is calm and feels safe, our mind becomes clear. When we're regulated, we operate within what psychologist Dr. Dan Siegel calls the Window of Tolerance[3], the optimal range of arousal where we can stay engaged, present, and effective under pressure. Inside this window, our nervous system can handle stress without tipping into overwhelm or shutting down. Step outside this window, however, and our body either speeds up into fight-or-flight or collapses into fatigue. Regulation allows us to widen our "Window of Tolerance" so that pressure doesn't knock us off center.

Bottom line: we cannot "mindset" our way out of stress or ignore it and carry on with business as usual. When stress isn't addressed, it starts to leak into everything: low energy, short patience, restless sleep, shallow breathing, and a feeling of always being "on edge." Over time, this stress response quietly erodes our ability to think clearly, decide wisely, and lead with intention.

Returning to Stability

Regulation interrupts that loop. It gives us the capacity to notice when we're drifting into threat mode and allows us to return to stability before it defines our behavior. The intention here is not to be calm all the time. Some stress is actually healthy and necessary, for example the feeling we get when working to submit a deliverable by a certain

---

[3] *Siegel, D. J. (1999).* The Developing Mind: Toward a Neurobiology of Interpersonal Experience.

deadline. The pressure in this case is motivating and helps us get there. The intention of regulation is to increase our window of tolerance and be flexible enough to come back to our center when high pressure spikes.

You've probably noticed in tense situations that the calmest person in the room often holds the most influence, and they come across as more confident. Regulation changes how we show up and how we behave and think. It allows for a grounded presence others can feel and trust. As a leader of your organization, your calmness allows people to be calm themselves, to be relaxed, and not worried or on alert, as they know it is safe to open up, to speak their mind, and contribute meaningfully. Energy is infections. After interacting with you people will either sense the calm confident presence, or they'll be on high alert themselves. So, what impression do you want to leave? The choice is yours!

I learned this the hard way. When I first started my business, people used to joke that I looked like a madman walking. I didn't see it at the time. Between client commitments, managing trades, suppliers, and constant deadlines, my tolerance for mistakes was nonexistent. Proud of the work I was doing, I wanted everything to run smoothly, with the precision of a Swiss watch. When the inevitable inconveniences happened, I was snapping at vendors and team members left and right, which I soon realized was not a sustainable way to work.

What changed was my desire to address the burnout and regain the energy lost from the constant stress. Even though, if I'm honest, some people did deserve being yelled at—they called it in!

To recap, when you **REGULATE**, you can face the same chaos, but with far more calm; you regain access to foresight, creativity, and empathy as your brain shifts out of threat mode and back into what is referred to as "executive functioning."

Inside the Resilient in Business OS™, we go deeper to help you build your regulation practice, one that anchors you with clarity, composure, and control, no matter what the business demands.

Regulation is the first ROOT for a reason. Dysregulation is detrimental to your entrepreneurial resilience, because it affects your judgement and, in turn, your actions. Over time, it can also push founders toward unhealthy coping mechanisms, often in the form of compulsive behaviors or addictions, which opens an entirely different challenge.

Next up, we will cover OBSERVE, where you'll learn the significance of recognizing the mental loops and stories that quietly drive your actions and might be holding your business back.

But before we move on, take a moment to reflect:
- What situations or patterns consistently push you into stress, urgency, or overdrive?

- How does dysregulation show up in your body: through tension, disrupted sleep, shallow breathing, irritability, or emotional volatility?

- When you feel off-center, what actually helps you reset mentally, physically, or emotionally (not what you think *should* help, but what truly does)?

- When was the last time you made an important decision from a stressed or exhausted state? Looking back, how did that affect the quality of the decision?

- Notice how much of your leadership happens from urgency, tension, or strain. If this became your default operating state for another year, how will this affect your mental health? And what do you sense it would cost you, not in output, but in clarity, presence, and stability?

CHAPTER 5
OBSERVE

Identify and Dismantle the Patterns
That Hold You Back

Does it sometimes feel like even though you are trying to do all of the right things, your business is not moving forward? You've tried all of the strategies, you've exhausted all the options you know about, you are doing your best, yet you still feel like you are stuck at a certain ceiling, not sure why and what is required to step out.

Every founder carries invisible habits, assumptions, and mental distortions that are not serving them positively, and yet that are quietly influencing how they make decisions. Most of the time, it is old programming that steers their decisions and sabotages their success, without their permission.

OBSERVE is about stepping out of autopilot mode and noticing what's happening. Instead of getting pulled into stories like "this is how it is supposed to be," or "I can't find the right people," or "I can't be charging this much!" we start identifying patterns holding us back and hearing those thoughts as signals.

Once we see the pattern, we can assess how it is serving us, then choose something different. Observation is the first step towards breaking that cycle. It allows you to confront, understand, and, ultimately, rewrite your inner narrative. It slows the noise long enough for us to think clearly, choose wisely, and break the loop that is not helping us move forward.

As you progress on the entrepreneurial journey, you realize what you're great at, what you enjoy doing, and what you carry resistance towards. The resistance may surprise you. It results from the part of your brain that is wired to keep you safe. Even when you know deep down that this is what you're here to do, a part of you might hold onto the familiar past and start to resist and sabotage the success you say you want.

Any resistance you may feel is internally rooted, as there might still be a conflict in identity between the version of you reaching forward and the one afraid to let go of what has been familiar. People often blame external forces—competition, the economy, the industry, or clients—for their circumstances. However, the response to what is happening in the external world is a reflection of our internal world and subsequently the results obtained.

This is where you can be your only competition. Nothing holds you back other than your own beliefs and your resistance to your new identity. Even after saying *yes* to your dream, on a deeper level you might still not see yourself in the role of success at that level, and you might subconsciously doubt that success is a possible outcome for you. This becomes evident when you procrastinate, hesitate to fully commit, or work in a way that doesn't help your business move forward.

When your self-identity is not fully aligned with the identity of the person that carriers the level of success you are aiming for, that misalignment manifests in the decisions you make, in the action you take, and in how you show up:

- You end up playing small because you're afraid of being judged

- You hide and avoid putting yourself out there

- You hold back on promoting your business the way you should

- You prevent yourself from fully investing in what will move your business forward

- You spend time being busy but not productive

- You do not make the right connections and business alliances

- You jump from one tactic to another hoping the next shiny object is the solution, without focusing on the real bottleneck

And then you wonder why you are not getting the results you had hoped.

Many subconscious factors can lead to self-sabotage: fear of failure, fear of success (which is more common than fear of failure of entrepreneurs), and imposter syndrome, as well as a sense of not feeling ready, not being enough, or not deserving.

When I first started my general contracting business, I made the mistake of doing everything myself for far longer than I'd like to admit. I delayed hiring, avoided delegation, wore all the hats. But the truth was, I was operating from a drive for perfection compounded by a fear of letting go and a fear of success. I was motivated by the excitement of finally being my own boss and building beautiful homes for people to the highest possible standard. Coming from an engineering background and caring about the environment led me down the rabbit hole of learning about and becoming certified in the highest available "green" building standards. I wanted people to live in comfortable, healthy, and beautiful spaces. Being a business owner was new, and not yet fully integrated into my identity, and this cost me profit, time, and the ability to scale faster.

I still remember when I signed my first client. It was a significant full-home remodeling project that involved structural alterations and an addition. I was happy the client had chosen me. It felt like I was finally in business. However, for some reason I felt a little sad for the competition. As the scope of work increased, I found myself resisting charging what the work should actually cost. I was constantly giving discounts to help the client. This had never been the case when I was doing similar projects while working for someone else, and it definitely is not a strategy recommended for anyone who wants to stay in business. It became clear I had a self-worth issue that hadn't been evident before. I knew I couldn't leave it unaddressed if I wanted to build a sustainable business.

As entrepreneurs we often forget how much we already know, and we underestimate the value we provide. What we do becomes second nature, we might assume others have the same knowledge and experiences, so we sell ourselves short. If you're providing exceptional service and still repeatedly undercharging, it's worth questioning what are you worried about and why haven't you really set your prices right. Is a self-worth problem at work here, or is it something else? It could be anything, really. Turns out us humans are very complicated, and there is no one-size-fits-all answer to our problems. It is important to note here that when we don't charge in alignment with the value we provide, we create an imbalance of energy that never ends well.

A New Addition

Alex and Emma's project is one I'm particularly proud of. I first met them at a tradeshow back in 2022. I was invited to visit their home shortly afterward to provide a consultation for their addition project. They weren't ready at the time to start with the work immediately. Fast forward two years, and they called out of the blue. After a few introductory exchanges, they got to the point:

"We had to postpone starting our renovation project a few times for different reasons. We're ready now, and the permit was just issued last week. We've decided to go ahead with the addition at the back of the house and a full main floor remodel. We're thinking of starting the work in about four months. Are you still interested?"

"Yes, absolutely. Feel free to send the plans, and I'll reach out with a proposal shortly."

This call happened right at the peak of the personal storm I described in Chapter 1. It was one of those moments where you realize that if something is meant for you, it will find you. That God does exist! Ironically, this has been the case over and over again. Just when about to give up, the mysterious hand of God shows up to indicate, "not yet, not today!" I recently heard the saying "There are no atheists in foxholes," and it resonated deeply. When all options seem exploited, surrender and faith in a higher power become the most evident path forward.

I took my time quoting the project, and I was thrilled to be selected for it. I convinced Alex and Emma to start the project in the next two weeks instead of waiting four months as they had previously planned, and that moment became the turning point for me, a financial relief that formed the beginning of my comeback. It became the most profitable project I'd ever done, and with the easiest clients I'd ever worked with.

Sometimes the answer to increasing your self-worth lies in simply persevering and summoning the capacity for resilience that will allow you to keep going. Just keep a log of all the amazing things you've achieved and all the challenges you had previously overcome, and there you go, that's your proof for when you're in doubt! You need to do the work repeatedly until you eliminate doubt and build enough evidence that you are the best possible choice for the project—and that you are the best choice for supporting your clients on their transformative journey. For me, that is what made the difference between how I showed up and priced my first project in business, and in how I priced Alex and Emma's project, one of my most profitable.

When a new, more confident identity becomes cemented into your subconscious mind, you begin showing up differently; people can sense it and you start attracting more and better opportunities.

Working with a mentor or a coach can be a powerful way to identify and dismantle your blind spots. There is truth in the saying that "You can't solve a problem with the same thinking that created it." Often, a lack of results is not due to a lack of effort, it's just that you're too close to the problem to see the solution. A fresh perspective is exactly what's needed to help you break a cycle that does not serve or move you forward. This is why some coaches hire another coach to help them figure something out.

I've seen these internal struggles and others play out repeatedly with my coaching clients. Every stage in business requires a different mindset and approach. Surrounding yourself with a like-minded community, working with a coach with whom you truly resonate, or getting guidance and support from people who have walked the path can make all the difference.

While coaching provides insight, journaling is a powerful tool for venting, releasing the mental load, tapping into your intuition, and getting the answers you are seeking. Even if you are new to journaling, putting your thoughts in writing helps your brain recover from stress, and it allows you to reach a sense of freedom and relief as you process all that is happening.

Definitely Not Woo-Woo

I used to think mindset was just a buzzword people threw around to sound smart, or that it was some sort of a woo-woo idea. It is definitely not. What I've come to realize is that our thoughts can either limit us or set us free. Many people build false cages in their brains that limit what they perceive is possible and what is not. We all have a friend who immediately attempts to play down our ideas the moment we share them, or they revert to immediately identifying how impossibly difficult it will be to make our idea work ... and how it is just a terrible idea. You can't really blame them; their mind is not wrapped around how to successfully execute and they perceive anything new as a threat. They do not have the courage and self-belief to attempt anything near what you are considering. Thank them and drive on. The way *you* think about and approach your business makes the difference between success and stagnation.

When you see someone else achieving success, it is important to use that as inspiration to play bigger, to realize what's possible. Any negative feelings about success often come from people who do not feel capable themselves—they have a fixed or limited mindset where ego and fear, instead of possibility, dominate. Remember the friend we all have, referenced earlier—the one always doubtful of any possibility for success? Even if you were to hand them an exact blueprint guaranteed to make money, the dominant rhetoric in their brain would find a way to doubt it, and they would discourage you and themselves from taking action. This is all to say, do not let your story, or your family's legacy, be defined by your friends. I've had many similar conversations. People say "I missed this great opportunity a few years ago, because my friends did not want in. Had they agreed, we would have been farther ahead by now." You can't live by someone else's limitations or standards. That only keeps you stuck in victimhood and serves as an excuse for giving your power away to others. Broadcasting your plans serves no purpose other than opening yourself up to criticism and sabotaging your progress. Keep your plans guarded except from the people who are involved in helping you make them come to fruition.

But even when you stop listening to friends' negative inputs, when you filter out all the static, there's still one person you have to confront: yourself. Because sometimes the voice holding you back isn't "out there," it's inside your own head, expressing the subconscious patterns and thoughts that no longer serve you but are still running the show. It is important to commit to yourself, to be your own advocate, to take your power back, identify what no longer serves, and move forward with trust. Remember, you are the main character in your story. It is all about you. No one else will be more invested, your success matters, and you're responsible for making it happen.

Self-sabotage isn't always obvious. It might look like saying "yes" to too many things, leaving no energy for what matters most. It might involve hiding behind busywork instead of making bold moves. It might even masquerade as success itself—landing a big client, then subconsciously dropping the ball because, deep down, you don't feel ready for that amount of growth. Look for the destructive repeating pattern that is making you your own biggest obstacle.

Yes, we are all on the path of providing the best service possible while helping people thrive; however, it is important to be mindful that we are not self-sabotaging our way out of business at the same time.

Observation matters because self-awareness is the lever that gets you off the hamster wheel and shifts everything else in your business in the right direction. Seeing the loop that's holding you back is not always a straightforward task.

Observing is the first step back into intentional leadership. It's what moves you out of fear, habit, and insecurity and brings you back on track, breaking free from the loops holding you back.

When we **OBSERVE**, we start catching unhelpful loops before they take over. We recognize the stories we've outgrown. We no longer treat every thought as truth or let emotions quietly run the show.

The real blockers to our success are not usually the obvious ones. They're the unconscious fears, inherited beliefs, and emotional reflexes we've never stopped long enough to notice. Observation interrupts the autopilot. It creates space between stimulus and response and in that space, we get our power back and can choose differently.

Inside the Resilient in Business OS™, implementation program, founders begin to see what's really driving their reactions—the loops, triggers, and stories that shape how they lead and make decisions. OBSERVE provides a structured way to notice the patterns before they stall your progress. The result is a system that allows you to step out of the self-imposed limitations and patterns holding you back, to step off the hamster wheel and take your business to its next level.

In the next chapter we will cover OWN. Here is where I will invite you to build an identity that is congruent with your future self.

Before going there, take some time to reflect:
- What stories are you still telling yourself about success, failure, or your own worth, and how are they shaping your decisions?

- Where are you reacting out of fear (of judgment, loss, conflict, not being enough, etc.), rather than responding with clarity and intention?

- What pattern keeps repeating in your business, no matter how much effort you throw at it, and what might that reveal about how you operate?

- Where do you notice yourself delaying or avoiding decisions, even when you know something needs to change?

- Look at the stories and beliefs that surfaced above. If even one of them stayed unchallenged, how might it continue shaping the way you build, lead, and respond? What is the cost of repeating the unhelpful patterns?

CHAPTER 6
OWN

Strengthen Your Self-Authority,
Choose Consciously, and Build Momentum

We all know someone who wants to be an entrepreneur. They start something, hesitate, and never fully move forward. Years later, they're still "getting ready." Or they briefly step into a new venture, pull back, and then move on to something else, again and again.

For some, getting ready can take a very long time. It manifests as a never-ending journey of learning, trying to get their hands on information about everything, so they are fully prepared for the right time to launch and for the stars to align, because, in their mind, they have a belief that this is how you successfully execute without making mistakes.

On a conscious level, they are serious and intentional about becoming a business owner. This is the path they want to pursue. Subconsciously, however, their self-perception and identity haven't fully caught up yet.

A weak or underdeveloped self-perception for the role can show up in many ways without us realizing it. One common example is having a strong idea that shows real promise and immediately sharing it with everyone you know, driven by excitement and the desire to announce what you're about to do. In doing so, you open yourself up to scrutiny, opinions, and judgments from well-meaning "experts", friends and family with little-to-no experience in actually building what you are aiming to build. By the end of these conversations, you feel drained and less convinced your idea will work.

Sharing too much with the wrong people can be a subtle form of self-sabotage. Because they love us, friends and family are often experts at explaining why something won't work, especially when they've never attempted anything similar themselves. Waiting for external validation is a recipe for disaster. It means giving your power away to people that will never validate your path. It is important to find what is true to you, and give yourself the permission to follow your intuition.

A poor self-perception can also show up sometimes for relatively new business owners who don't fully put themselves out there and don't talk about their services because, on some level, they are either scared of success or still not convinced of their ability to pull it off or provide a successful service to their clients. So, they remain cautious, procrastinate, and don't fully step into what the role requires.

Being in the driver's seat as the owner is an immensely different experience than being anyone else on the team. When the motives for assuming that role are not strong enough, the tendency to drop out when inconveniences occur, or when the results do not come as quickly as expected, are high. This is when you see people quitting because they can't handle the pressure, often right before they start building momentum.

Chances are most of us had moments where we questioned: "What do we want out of this? Is all this hard work worth it? Why am I not where I'd like to be?" Maybe you've felt like you've lost touch with why you started your business or where you're going. Well, you're not alone: this questioning is common, especially during tough times, when we're working hard but not necessarily seeing the fruits of our labour. **OWN** is about coming back to yourself, taking full ownership of your path, of your successful founder identity, reconnecting with what truly drives you, and building aligned momentum towards your goals.

When your current identity is not in harmony with what your vision requires—where you'd like to be—you won't take the actions required to get you there. A quick example here is that a business owner running a team of fifty employees thinks and operates differently than the business owner with a team of two or three people. When you stop and consider the differences between those two versions of people, you realize the disconnect and that operating at a higher level requires new ways of being and a new version of you.

OWN plays a major role in your resilience as a founder. It allows you to remain connected with your values and truth which in turn allows you to remain motivated on this path despite all the chaos—to keep the bigger picture in mind, and to show up every day, even though you might not feel like it. This clarity allows you to know where to focus your energy and time; you will see any inconvenience along the way as just that, and you won't be easily swayed or tempted to change direction as a result of minor hurdles. The clarity becomes your compass, your north star, keeping you anchored into what matters and protecting you from being sidetracked, overcommitted, or fragile.

OWN is about reconnecting with the deeper "why" behind your work, the purpose that makes the struggle worth it, and the long-term vision that gives your effort direction. Ownership is knowing what you stand for and what truly drives you. This clarity becomes a filter to your decisions and a roadmap to your next steps.

Owning your direction means you stop waiting for external validation and approval from others to confirm you're on the right path. You move with internal knowing, with conviction, and you begin creating momentum from within. Ownership gives you a sense of inner authority that is not waiting for external permission or validation to move forward.

To OWN means:

- You know what matters, you are clear on where you are headed, and you take action towards it every day

- You focus on what keeps you motivated, despite daily challenges or inconveniences

- You take full responsibility for your path and how you show up

By contrast, when we don't own who we are, when we don't revert back to our truth, our business runs us. This is when we start chasing different opportunities that are not necessarily aligned. It's also when we say "yes" out of fear and confuse activity for progress. We get easily swayed and distracted off our path and any hurdle feels very heavy. We might look confident but we feel disconnected and we might not have a strong enough motive to tolerate the discomfort we are facing.

When we OWN who we are, everything changes. We make decisions from clarity, not anxiety. We say "no" to distraction because we know what deserves our "yes." We remain focused and lead our team with calm conviction—and people feel it. Ownership brings coherence as our thoughts, actions, and goals start pulling in the same direction.

For me, OWN has become the anchor that keeps me grounded and showing up every day. I tend to be motivated by big goals as I find it stimulating to be building and working towards something meaningful. OWN has become my daily reminder of where I want to be. It is where I map out my next steps, and plan the process of getting there. OWN allows me to stay connected to my direction. I stay motivated by coming back to my "why," to gratitude, and to my exciting vision. It allows me to build momentum and work towards those goals. My tolerance to pain increased, challenges along the way don't disappear, but I'm no longer defined by them, I am not discouraged by them and I am not distracted by shiny objects. Sometimes, our best moves are the actions we do not take. Nonetheless, we need to be true to ourselves and have that filter.

Your Legacy Begins with Ownership
Your legacy is what you live by every day and the impact you leave on the people around you. Ownership is where your legacy begins. It's the ripple of your presence, the standard you uphold, the way people feel after working with you, the trust your team builds under your leadership. It's in how you show up for yourself when no one's watching, and how your actions inspire others to do the same.

When we **OWN** who we are and show up true to ourselves, we make our lives easier. True ownership creates alignment, authority, and impact that outlasts any single achievement. It builds the legacy that lives through others long after our work is done.

The Resilient in Business OS™, helps you step into that aligned identity, so you can start building aligned momentum. When everything around you feels uncertain, being true to who you are keeps you steady.

Next, we move into TEND, where we'll focus on protecting your energy, and building a sustainable rhythm.

But before we do that, here are a few reflection questions:

- When things get hard, what truly fuels your drive, and what consistently drains it, even if you don't want to admit it?

- Where in your business are you leading from alignment (this feels like *you*), and where are fear, doubt, or pressure still making the decisions?

- What part of your vision have you been minimizing, postponing, or toning down in order to keep things stable or comfortable?

- If you fully owned your vision and trusted your ability to figure things out, what bold move would you make — and what would you walk away from?

- Notice what you've been minimizing or postponing in order to keep things predictable or comfortable. If you stopped compromising and resisting going all in, what would change?

CHAPTER 7
TEND

Optimize Your Energy and
Build Your Sustainable Rhythm

I've never been a gym person. I just couldn't care less about going to the gym. If you are, congratulations, I hope you're enjoying it and would be open to representing me there! I am more the being-active-in-nature kind of guy. I prefer to go for my run on the trail by my home, where I can hear the birds chirping, say "hi" to people, and enjoy the beautiful views.

Anyway, it is more or less common knowledge for people who work out that if you work on certain body parts one day, the next day you give those muscles a break and focus on something else. I guess this is referred to as rest and recovery days. This is as far as my gym knowledge goes. Yet as entrepreneurs, the pressure we feel can sometimes make us think we have to keep pushing all the time, at all costs. And the outcome: more stress, exhaustion, burnout, less productivity, poor decisions, neglect of all other areas of life. The list goes on ...

The side effects of the imbalance in how we spend our energy ripple beyond ourselves, even though in the moment we are so caught up in the problems at hand that we might not stop and question it. This has an impact on our business, our families, our team, and all relationships, really.

You've probably had seasons where you felt like the only way forward was to work harder, put in long nights, create endless to-do lists, and push through exhaustion because everything depended on you. There's a saying that entrepreneurs are the only people who will work eighty hours a week to avoid working forty hours a week. It's usually said half-jokingly, but it reveals something real: founders don't resist work, they resist constraint.

The problems arise when intensity becomes a permanent operating mode rather than a temporary phase that is optimized around your energy patterns. Grind at all costs feels like progress until we realize it puts us on the fast track to burnout.

The reality is that success is not a result of how much we can push. Success comes from working smarter, from following a sustainable rhythm that allows us to play the long game.

TEND is about reclaiming your energy through a sustainable rhythm. It's about learning to manage effort and recovery with intention, so you can perform at your best without burning out in the process. Pushing harder leads to depletion and ineffectiveness; your focus fragments, the quality of your decisions drops, and your energy leaks increase.

TEND is about building systems that help us manage our energy and recover faster. It is where you review your habits, keeping what serves and letting go of what doesn't, utilizing rest as a strategy that supports your productivity, and designing a rhythm which becomes your edge. The side benefit of this process is a calmer nervous system, as you invite predictability and safety to your schedule instead of living reactively in chaos.

It is not uncommon to be focused on different aspects of your business except the one system that fuels you: your energy. You can't lead effectively and be fully available for your team when your body, mind, and focus are out of sync. TEND is about mastering that sync. It's the practice of optimizing how you use, recover, and renew energy so you can operate in flow, so you are full of energy and high on creativity.

Many founders focus on time management and try to figure out how to be more "productive." A more effective strategy would be to manage your energy instead. This starts by conducting an energy audit, a review of how you spend your energy in the week. It is best to track this over a two-week period, in fifteen-minute increments. You can then determine where your energy is going—to which type of tasks—and identify which tasks are high value and you should continue doing, and which are activities someone else on the team could undertake. Filtering what should remain and what should be delegated ensures you stay focused on what actually moves your business forward.

TENDING to your energy means treating it like your most valuable asset. The more you manage your energy intentionally, the more predictable your performance becomes. We TEND across four dimensions:

- **Mind** — involves focus, thinking strategically, and prioritizing what matters to you

- **Heart** — is about staying emotionally grounded and connected

- **Body** — focuses on maintaining physical energy through movement, recovery, and rest

- **Spirit** — highlights staying aligned with your purpose and what gives your life meaning

After completing your energy audit and narrowing your focus to the activities that actually move the business forward, the next step is to design your week so you use your time intentionally. This includes:

- Applying proven time-management practices.

- Using time blocks.

- Grouping similar tasks together.

- Designating certain days with themes for specific types of work.

- Setting meetings at specific times.

- Setting boundaries with your team so you are not distracted, and

- Removing unnecessary interruptions.

- It also means scheduling space to respond to unexpected issues so they don't derail your entire day.

Scheduling breaks and time for rest and recovery are just as important as scheduling work and meetings. High performance isn't about pushing non-stop; it's about protecting your capacity. When you deliberately build white space into your week, you prevent cognitive fatigue, create space to calm your mind and think, and reset your nervous system.

Intentional pauses include short breaks between tasks, dedicated recovery time after demanding days, and having weekly reset rituals where you can shift focus and enjoy life. This rhythm is what will keep you motivated to work hard, and showing up energetic and ready to take over the world!

For me, TENDING means integrating work and life in a way that I enjoy. It's about scheduling time for exercise every morning, eliminating noise during designated focus time, and blocking time to have some fun. It also means setting aside time to respond to chaos—the unexpected things that demand attention—so they don't derail my flow. It's about creating a rhythm in my calendar that helps me stay effective and centered. It's about delegating tasks I don't enjoy and making space for long walks where new ideas can—and do—emerge.

Entrepreneurs often believe their biggest constraint is time and many say they don't have enough of it. But the true constraint is energy. When your energy is fragmented, you show up depleted, your interest starts to fade; you end up feeling exhausted all the time, doing low value work without realizing it. Your team can sense this and, make no mistake: they are affected by it. The result is that you end up running around in circles and not really moving your business forward as effectively as you could.

Inside the Resilient in Business OS™, we identify where the energy leaks are and design a sustainable and enjoyable rhythm that helps founders become truly effective while experiencing true freedom.

In summary, **TENDING** to your energy supports sustainable performance, and allows you to adopt a rhythm that results in properly integrating work and life in your schedule, and not burning out along the way. Next up, we will cover SUPPORT, where we build the systems, relationships, and structures that make your business more reliable and provide the best leverage.

Before we do that, here a few reflective questions:

- Where is your energy being drained right now, and are you ignoring the cost?

- Which part of you—mind, heart, body, or spirit—have you been neglecting the most?

- What would change if you built a sustainable rhythm and managed your energy intentionally, if you had just 20% more mental and emotional bandwidth?

- If you designed a rhythm that was sustainable for the next 3–5 years, what would need to shift in how you work, rest, and recover?

- If your current rhythm continued without adjustment, would it support the version of you that's trying to emerge, or slowly pull you away from it?

CHAPTER 8
SUPPORT

Build Your Winning Ecosystem

John, one of my clients, owned a marketing business that employed about forty people. The business had been in the family for about fifteen years and he had an operator running it, which had allowed him to step away over the last couple of years to pursue other interests. He was happy not to be involved, but the one issue he couldn't ignore was that the company was breaking even, over and over again. The operator was running it with the primary concern of protecting his role. The operation was a mess, client information was scattered, everything was tied to that single person and had to be processed through him, and, not surprisingly, they were losing out on many opportunities and profitability was not a priority.

It was obvious the situation was a struggle for John. On one side, he was happy that he was not involved in the day-to-day; on the other side, he knew breaking even was just not right. I mean, what's the point? Another struggle was that he needed to confront the chaos, deal with the operator, and let go.

The beauty of entrepreneurship is that it can be done in many different ways, there are many different types of entrepreneurs: the small business owners, lifestyle entrepreneurs, serial entrepreneurs, the enterprise builders, etc. There's no right or wrong way to do it. What matters is choosing a path that fits your goals and supports a life you genuinely enjoy. The real difference between a solopreneur and a founder building an enterprise isn't necessarily talent or ambition. It's leverage. The solopreneur grows through personal effort and is limited by what they can individually produce in the time they have. The enterprise builder utilizes leverage through people, systems, and structure so they can make a larger impact. One depends on personal endurance and feels like fighting an uphill battle by yourself; the other depends on a reliable ecosystem that provides support and freedom.

Every founder is in the game for different reasons but the two kinds of freedom they typically crave relate to time and money. Time freedom in business doesn't come from doing everything yourself, it comes from designing the right support around you. The founders who scale sustainably minimize risk by surrounding themselves with the right support ecosystem, they infuse resilience into what they are building by getting out of the lone-wolf mindset and inviting the right people to be part of the journey.

In John's case, his support ecosystem needed lots of optimizing. That's the intent behind the fifth root, SUPPORT. It's about building an ecosystem that protects your time, multiplies your capacity, and strengthens your business's ability to thrive without being dependent on you alone.

The previous dimensions—REGULATE, OBSERVE, OWN, and TEND— focus on you and on encouraging you to let go of what sabotages and holds your business back, but **SUPPORT** is about designing the next level of your entrepreneurial resilience. It allows you to build a business that is more reliable, and that is not dependent on key personnel or your constant day-to-day input to be functional. SUPPORT is the layer that moves you from building with intensity to strategic leverage and reliability.

Founders are wired to solve problems and take responsibility, which comes with the territory and most take great pride in doing; they also master the art of the juggle. But that strength can easily turn into isolation. You've probably heard the saying, "It's lonely at the top." Being in charge and consumed with the day-to-day minutia sometimes leads founders to neglect surrounding themselves with the right support network; they don't ask for help, and they become disconnected from those who could offer valuable perspective and feedback.

SUPPORT is the infrastructure we intentionally design and nurture. It keeps us grounded when we need it most and it makes our businesses more reliable. It also means we can access the help we need when we experience uncertain times. When properly implemented, SUPPORT allows growth without chaos.

You need four types of SUPPORT:

1. **Personal Support** — this is about your personal resilience. As we said before, your business is all about you. Before reaching for outside assistance, it's important to support yourself first through routines, a sustainable work rhythm, good recovery habits, and boundaries that protect your time and energy. Everything that was covered earlier in: REGULATE, OBSERVE, OWN and TEND.

2. **Relational Support** — this includes the members of your trusted inner circle who provide emotional support. The people who see you, challenge you, and remind you that you're loved and not alone (your family, friends, and other members of your close trusted circle).

3. **Operational Support** — this relates to your internal leverage in the business and includes your direct team—the people helping you deliver your product or service. Here it is important to define clear roles, delegate ownership and ensure accountability is in place. It's also important, operationally, that you have clear workflows, processes and systems, set communication rhythms and ensure you are not dependent on key personnel in order to reduce your business risk. We might be on the verge of interfering with the territory of business operating systems here, a little bit, however, we are going to cross that line anyway in the name of entrepreneurial resilience, building a well-oiled operation and leaning on proper structure and operational support. These all ultimately allow you to sleep better at night, achieve more with less resources, increase business reliability and yield a direct positive effect on your sanity, freedom, and profit, the entire point of this exercise.

4. **Strategic Support** — this is about your external network: mentors, coaches, consultants, advisors, your referral network, your partners, alliances, and industry peers who care for and promote your business. The members of your strategic support network help you expand your perspective, keep you updated about new trends in your industry, help you identify and address your blind spots, and are ultimately your advocates. This is the trusted group of people you align with and who are motivated to help you succeed.

We've all heard the saying, "Success is about who you know, not what you know." And the longer I'm in business, the truer that statement becomes. Knowing how to build the right support ecosystem requires great execution skills and can make a tremendous difference between stagnation and success.

Coming from the construction world, I've experienced firsthand how the relationships I built in my support network have saved me repeatedly. General contracting is, at its core, a people business. Without trusted relationships, you can only go so far. I've had countless moments over the years when my back was against the wall but because of the people I had surrounded myself with—the trust and relationships I had built over the years—I was able to resolve my problems.

Those relationships weren't built by accident; they were built through experience, trust, and mutual respect. As simple as it sounds, when you treat people well, connect genuinely, and lead with your heart and with integrity, people want to work with you. They want to be part of your team. And when things get tough, they'll do everything they can to help.

All of this may sound obvious when said out loud, but it is surprising how many people get it wrong. I always hear stories of founders who haven't been appreciating the people around them. They've forgotten that relationships, and not transactions, are what truly hold a business together.

If you want to build resilience in your business, waiting until you need help and are stretched too thin to seek support is a terrible strategy; it is important to design your support network early on, and nurture it continuously. Your business is only as strong as the ecosystem supporting it. SUPPORT multiplies your capacity in five ways:

1. It protects your time, energy, and mental bandwidth so you can focus on high-value decisions.

2. It removes dependency on key personnel and provides leverage as you empower others to lead, take ownership, and grow with the business. This leads to a more reliable operation.

3. It allows you to step out of the day-to-day firefighting and work on your business.

4. It drives sustainable growth by aligning people, systems, and priorities toward a shared vision.

5. It connects you with reliable people and trusted allies you can lean on when things get challenging.

In the Resilient in Business OS™, SUPPORT is where resilience expands beyond us. It's about creating the ecosystem that provides leverage and business reliability, and sustains growth.

Next, we'll bring everything together inside your Resilient in Business OS™, the framework that unites all five ROOTS into one integrated rhythm.

Before moving on, though, here are a few reflection questions:

- What kind of support — from people, systems, or structure — would free you to think, create, and lead at a higher level?

- Where are you still trying to carry things that should be shared, delegated, automated, or released altogether?

- Which decisions still land on your desk by default, even though they don't actually require your level of expertise?

- What needs to change in the next 6 – 12 months, to design a business that supports your freedom, and not just the other way around?

CHAPTER 9
YOUR RESILIENT IN
BUSINESS OS™

Lead with Structure,
Sustainable Rhythm, and Momentum

When the external world is beyond your control, focusing on yourself, on what *is,* means working on what supports your entrepreneurial resilience—what helps you remain deeply rooted and supported, as you show up consistently and build your legacy.

Every scalable, professionally managed business runs on systems: sales, marketing, operations, finance, HR, and more. The most effective founders don't stop there. They realize that sustainable growth requires building systems for themselves. This is critical, knowing how much the results of a small business are influenced by how founders lead themselves and their businesses.

The Resilient in Business OS™ gives you, the founder, the infrastructure to build capacity and the strength required to respond to uncertainty and move your small business out of stagnation into its next level. This personal operating system is a custom framework designed to help you get out of your own way and position your business for the next level. As we've been seeing in previous chapters, it's built on the five ROOTS of Entrepreneurial Resilience:

- **REGULATE** — Master your internal state and cultivate strong presence, composure, and discernment

- **OBSERVE** — Identify and dismantle the patterns holding you back

- **OWN** — Lead from alignment, anchor into your inner authority, and build momentum fearlessly

- **TEND** — Optimize your energy and build your sustainable rhythm

- **SUPPORT** — Build your winning ecosystem

Each of the ROOTS are practices vital to supporting you in leading yourself effectively, and your business by extension. They help you increase your entrepreneurial resilience and support you in playing the long-term game. Understanding the ROOTS conceptually is a good start, but the transformation only happens when you apply them on a daily basis; just like any system in your business.

REGULATE is your *stabilization system.* It's what allows you to stay calm under pressure and lead from presence, not panic. The result creates a ripple effect on the people around you as they feel safer opening up to you and confident in you. Without this foundation, every challenge you meet feels like an emergency, your energy levels remain low, and you just can't think straight or sustain the proper mindset to make the right decisions.

OBSERVE is your *awareness system*. It gives you visibility into your own patterns and behaviors so you can catch the loops you keep repeating and the beliefs that don't serve you but are driving your decisions. Without breaking the loops sabotaging your success, no strategy can prevail.

OWN is your *alignment, motivation and momentum building system*. When you OWN who you are and where you're going, you stop chasing distractions, you stop being easily swayed by the external world, and you start leading with conviction. This system anchors you into what motivates you even though you might feel you want to quit at times. It connects your daily actions back to your deeper why—to your desired identity and vision—as you set your goals and work towards them.

TEND is your *energy optimization system*. It keeps your performance renewable. By managing effort and recovery intentionally, you remain consistent, creative, and in flow, rather than falling into the trap of becoming frequently distracted or burning out.

SUPPORT is your *leverage system*. It expands your capacity through people, structure, and collaboration. This is where your impact becomes scalable. Once you've mastered how to lead yourself, in SUPPORT you design the ecosystem that amplifies your impact, enables your business to become more reliable, and provides you with true freedom.

When all five systems are working together, they form a personal operating system that keeps you internally grounded and on the right path. You shift from impulsively managing chaos to operating strategically with rhythm.

Infusing Resilience into Your Business Beyond the ROOTS Framework

After getting the right support ecosystem in place, it's important to ensure you are building a winning culture in your organization, a place where your team enjoys working and everyone feels like they belong. Better still is when everyone is rallied around the vision and is excited about their contribution to the business's success. When everyone is on board with where you are heading, and is looking for ways to get you there, your job becomes significantly easier.

Following the theme of this book, you might have predicted by now what I am about to say next: you, the founder, play a major role in defining the culture of your organization. You play a major role in making sure the team is on board with the company's values and they are embodying them in their daily interaction with each other and with clients. You play a major role in creating what is referred to as psychological safety, the team's ability to speak up, express their thoughts, their ideas and concerns safely without fear of judgement. You play a major role in ensuring that everyone feels like their contributions are being seen and are valued, and that they belong. All of the above, does not necessarily carry a line item on the profit and loss statement, and can't necessarily be quantified in terms of dollar value, however, they have a direct impact on your business. This is what determines how excited people are about working with you, how motivated they are to help you achieve your vision, which translates to how your team treats your clients and how your clients are satisfied with your service.

I have seen the effects of a toxic culture over and over again: team members who are pushy with clients or who show up to their work in a way that makes it obvious they don't care. This is why it is important to actively monitor that part of the business and work toward building a winning culture instead.

We can't talk about entrepreneurial resilience without quickly covering the topic of risk mitigation. Yes, certain events are beyond our control and we can't predict everything, however, as founders it is our responsibility to attempt to anticipate and quantify the impact of potential bottlenecks, blind spots, and whatever else might go wrong. I can speak from personal painful experiences here. Risk mitigation is often overlooked, as we are busy with our day-to-day demands, responding to fires, or pursuing our next goal. However, the more diligent we are in identifying any potential problems before they occur, the better we can plan, and the more prepared and resilient our businesses will become. Risk can exist in all areas of business, so basically all areas should be examined. One example can be looking at existing vendors. Are you overly dependent on one supplier that is critical to your pipeline? What happens when that supplier cannot deliver, or when their prices go up significantly higher? Does it make sense to open lines of communication with others as well?

In the Resilient in Business OS™ implementation program, we dive deeper into those topics and guide you through them as we cover what it looks like to lead your team when facing major challenges—what to do and what not to do—so you can navigate with greater confidence.

Outcomes of The Resilient in Business OS™ implementation include:

1. You Lead Yourself with Stability Instead of Stress
The way you operate changes from reacting to urgencies to remaining grounded under pressure, thinking clearly, and making decisions from a stable state rather than from emotional spikes.

2. You Break Old Patterns and Lead with Awareness
You catch loops like overthinking, perfectionism, avoidance, people-pleasing, micromanaging, and urgency before you react from old programming. This allows you to escape the loops that are holding you back.

3. You Build Conviction and Direction

You reconnect with who you are, what you care about, and where you're headed. Your actions become deliberate. Instead of drifting and giving up early when pressure hits, you remain motivated and build momentum.

4. You Build a Sustainable Rhythm That Prevents Burnout

Your energy stabilizes, you spend more time in flow, and you focus on the work that actually moves things forward. You also recover faster and stop wasting energy on low-value tasks.

5. You Create a Support Ecosystem That Multiplies Your Capacity

You're no longer the bottleneck. You build personal, relational, operational, and strategic support that reduces risk in the business and frees you to lead more strategically.

6. You Make Better Decisions Faster

You filter out the noise and your decisions become aligned with what is true for you.

7. You Gain Emotional Bandwidth and Leadership Presence

People respond to your calm and confidence. You create psychological safety, communicate more effectively, and lead without pressure leaking through.

8. You Lead Confidently Through Uncertainty and Mitigate Risk

You hone the skill of leading and motivating your team in times of crisis. You anticipate issues before they arise and prepare for them.

9. You Become More Resilient

Challenges don't knock you off center anymore. You recover quickly, respond with intention, and stay grounded during setbacks.

10. You Build the Infrastructure to Scale with Clarity Instead of Chaos

ROOTS becomes your internal infrastructure—your system for effective leadership and strategic moves.

As founders, leading effectively is not a choice when our plan is to create meaningful impact and remain in this game and win. If you are curious about the implementation of the Resilient in Business OS™ and are ready to escape survival mode and put yourself in the driver's seat of your growing business, reach out and book your personal operating system audit. This is an opportunity to identify what is working and what is not, where blind spots exist that sabotage your success, and which pain points need to be addressed to support your business's next stage of growth. To book your audit, visit www.resilientinbusiness.com

Now let's dive into how to embody resilience and build your winning legacy despite any challenges or setbacks.

Before we go there, it is time for reflection:

- When pressure, uncertainty, or setbacks hit, can you reliably stay grounded and think clearly, or does stress still hijack your leadership more than you'd like to admit?

- Are you recognizing and interrupting self-sabotaging patterns in real time, or mostly running on autopilot and only seeing them in hindsight?

- Is your way of working creating sustainable momentum, or quietly relying on intensity, overextension, and personal sacrifice?

- If you stepped away for thirty days, would your business operate reliably, or would stress, confusion, and reactivity take over?

PART THREE

EMBODYING RESILIENCE AND BUILDING YOUR LEGACY

CHAPTER 10
YOUR UNDERRATED
COMPETITIVE ADVANTAGE

Give Yourself a Break.
Embrace Self-Compassion, Grace, and Rest.

As a driven founder, you might have the tendency to keep pushing no matter what, especially when you are not seeing the results you expected. Over time, it's easy to lose track of how much you're actually doing, as you get caught up solving problems and trying to figure out your next move. When you don't see immediate results, you might start feeling overwhelmed, or guilty that you're not doing enough ... even when you're already doing more than most.

The weight builds quietly: constant stress, endless responsibilities, high expectations. If you're being honest, you might start questioning how much longer you can maintain this pace. The truth? That voice in your head, the one saying, "You should be further by now," isn't always right.

You might be telling yourself you have to keep your foot on the pedal, that you will rest "later," after you solve this problem, or reach that next goal. The problem is that in many cases, "later" never comes.

I know from personal experience; I used to get offended when someone told me to "take it easy." What do you mean, *take it easy*? This is what working looks like. What do *you* know? And how dare you question how I work?!

The drive to succeed comes from something deeply personal: providing a great service, honoring a vision, rewriting a family story, breaking generational patterns, or even just feeling determined to prove that you can make it. That kind of motivation can turn into self-imposed pressure to be performing at your best at all times. You might wear exhaustion like a badge, believing it's the trademark of success, a sign that you are working hard.

The truth is, working your way to depletion is not what success looks like. It is definitely not a recommended strategy if you plan to remain in this game for the long term. To be resilient in business you need continuity. For that, it is important to follow a rhythm that includes rest, reflection, and re-centering.

Burnout can happen for many reasons—doing work you are not in full alignment with or not excited about, for example. When you're not realizing the results you expected it's easy to feel de-motivated, which makes doing the work even harder.

Operating in chaos can also cause burnout. Having to deal with multiple competing demands that keep piling up over time makes for very heavy emotional and mental lifting. Eventually you can find yourself overwhelmed and at the point where you have had enough.

If something doesn't shift, your business will suffer and you will run yourself down. It took me a long time to learn that the answer to overwhelm isn't always doing more or thriving until further notice. It was also tough for me to finally get that slowing down is not failure or weakness but rather it's absolutely necessary for simplifying, processing, and coming back to the game feeling more energized and excited about the work you're doing in the world.

There's a common belief that being tough, disciplined, and hard on yourself is what keeps you on track to achieve your goals. From there, some people conclude that external pressure, such as accountability partners who yell at you, is the solution. In other words, they choose motivation through force. This approach may work for a while. But when pressure is the only driver, progress eventually depends on finding an even bigger stick to keep going. Over time, this becomes exhausting and unsustainable.

What if the opposite is true? Research in psychology shows that individuals who practice self-compassion demonstrate greater resilience, recover quicker from setbacks, regulate stress more effectively, and experience a stronger internal sense of psychological safety[4].

Self-compassion doesn't make you soft. It is essential to creating enough space between what is happening to pause, assess the situation and choose a response rather than be driven by pressure.

Mental Breaks

There are different ways you can show yourself some compassion. The first is to take mental breaks. Mental breaks help you stop the spiral and gain some perspective about what's actually on your plate. Create a list of everything you are dealing with. For each item on that list note if it is within your control, or not. Where are you carrying weight that no one else can see? What would you say to a friend who was managing everything you are? For some reason, we tend to be more understanding and forgiving when talking to our friends and more critical when speaking to ourselves. Remind yourself that today is not the entire story.

---

[4] Kristin Neff, K. D., K. L. Kirkpatrick, and S. S. Rude, "The relationship between self-compassion and adaptive psychological functioning," *Journal of Research in Personality*, Volume 41, No. 1, (February 2007): 139–154.

This exercise helps you realize the magnitude of all that you are managing, and it can help you justify taking time to rest—if you need help justifying that. But more than that, it will help you become more aware of all the things that you are dealing with, and this is the first step in lightening your load. Some problems are not within your control but are causing self-imposed pressure anyway. Perhaps they can come off your list of to-dos. And, once you do see how much you are actually *rightfully* trying to accomplish, that might just give you the impetus to get better at delegation.

Generally speaking, awareness invites you to stop being so hard on yourself. Clarity on your next steps does not usually show up when you are living in chaos; it often shows up when you stop forcing it: during a quiet walk, in meditation, in the moments you allow yourself to just be.

Emotional Breaks

Another way to show yourself self-compassion is by taking emotional breaks. Feeling anger, doubt, joy, fear ... none of that makes you weak. The problem with negative emotions is that they do not just go away magically. They dwell in the background until further notice, and as a result consume our thoughts, our mental bandwidth, more than we might prefer. It is important to process those negative feelings to ensure you do not keep dwelling on them in endless loops for long periods of time. After naming your emotions, process and release them by talking to a trusted friend or counselor, or through meditation, breathwork, or journaling.

Structural Breaks

The third type of breaks critical for self-compassion are structural breaks. Think recovery time after a big week: white space in your calendar that is not filled with to-dos. Set boundaries to protect your peace, take a simple Sunday reset or find another day that works best for you—just take a day off when you need it, or go on a short vacation every few months. Making compassion and intentional reset time a part of your rhythm helps boost your creativity and allows you to be more productive. Regular structural breaks prevent cumulative stress and help in sustaining your long-term energy.

The core message here and throughout the entire book is this: *allow yourself to be human.* Give yourself some grace to thrive. Realize that as terrible as the situation can get, beating the same drum repeatedly is not the answer and will not help you move forward. You do not have to wait until you are completely burnt out to realize you are overextended. You do not have to prove your worth to anyone or to yourself by pushing past your limits. In fact, one of the most powerful things you can do is to recognize when you are overwhelmed, and to give yourself a break. When that happens, slow down and choose to step back. This is the high-return reset required to coming back fresh, energized, and ready to make your next impactful move.

You Need Some Space

Leading from resilience starts with becoming aware of the magnitude of what you are carrying and following that with a willingness to say: "This is a lot. I need space. I need help. I need to set boundaries. I'm doing the best I can. I need a vacation, a walk (etc.)." The space you create will help you gain clarity and find creative solutions that are realized from peace and not from a place of panic or fear.

I remember talking to a coach I had at one point and saying something along the lines of, "I just want to be successful." He immediately stopped me and said, "What are you talking about? You already *are* successful. Can't you see how far you have come?" What is interesting about the entrepreneurial journey—and this is a pitfall that many fall into—is that we have such big plans, and we're so focused on achieving one thing after another, that we tend to overlook everything we've already accomplished. You might be walking around focused on your next goal without having defined what success actually looks like to you. Recognize those "mid-term" successes and celebrate them along the way!

If today you feel like you're running on empty, give yourself permission to breathe, rest, and recover. You do not need anyone else's permission; you are the boss, after all! Let this chapter be your sign to book that vacation, lay down on a beach for a week or two, and have some fun.

If your business slows down the moment you step away, or you're constantly worried that everything depends on you, it's time to fix that. Reach out, and I'll help you get out of the weeds and build the structure that sets you free. In the meantime, take the damned vacation. You'll thank yourself later. Life's too short to build a business that traps you. The real goal is freedom—so you can serve your vision, live your purpose, and create a business that works for you ... not the other way around.

Sometimes, we try to be "mentally strong" and push through, ignoring what we're really experiencing; this can be dangerous as it disconnects us from our truth and keeps us stuck in survival mode.

In the next chapter, we'll bring it all together. We'll reconnect with the bigger picture, with what it truly means to lead from your core, provide a roadmap to winning, navigating uncertainty, and building your legacy.

Before we do that, however, here are some questions for reflection:

- What have you been carrying, minimizing, normalizing, or pushing through without truly acknowledging its true weight?

- Which pressures are you feeling right now that are actually within your control, and which ones aren't?

- What signals have your body or mind been sending that indicate it's time to slow down, reset, or create space— and how long have you been ignoring them?

- What would shift in your leadership, and in your decisions, if you gave yourself full permission to rest and reorient — not as an escape, but as an investment in your capacity?

CHAPTER 11
BUILDING YOUR WINNING LEGACY

Navigate Challenges and Find the Right Next Step

E ntrepreneurship takes us on a journey of self-discovery and tests us in ways other experiences can't. It reveals how we lead, plan, deploy resources, and navigate demands. It shows how much we're willing to learn and evolve and how committed we are to ourselves, to building our vision.

Along the way, our legacy is being built through every part of that journey. It is built and defined by how we show up, how we treat others, and how others perceive us. The moments that test us the most play a major role in defining our legacy. Our legacy is built not through our wins, but through how we define our story and how we hold ourselves when everything feels like it's falling apart.

The stress we feel when we stay in a demanding situation and hold tightly to our chaos drains our energy and can be paralyzing. This makes it nearly impossible to move forward, even when we would love to do so. It's important to get rid of the energy leakage that the pressure creates so we can salvage what is left of the situation and forge ahead. Sometimes, you haven't exhausted all your options and you just need some clarity and a little more persistence over time to build momentum and harvest the result of your labor. But when you find yourself in a prolonged set of uncertain circumstances, and you've exhausted all options, then it might be time to consider letting go. Surrendering and accepting the unfortunate "setback" is sometimes a powerful way to find your way forward.

Guilt or shame might be present, especially when things don't go as planned and the people around you are watching. Some may not be aligned with your goals; they might even be waiting to see you struggle, because it justifies their own fears or their lack of action. There's nothing shameful about the path you are walking. Taking action, building your future, and following the path to freedom is courageous. There's nothing shameful about going through uncertainty, missteps, or setbacks along the way. Some events may be unfortunate, but they're all part of the game. At least you're not walking through this lifetime mindlessly, and you're not terrified of believing in yourself. It takes courage to pursue freedom and most people are too afraid to pursue that goal. Celebrate your courage!

Your interpretation of any event at a particular moment depends on how your mind perceives it. What might look like an unfortunate event or a setback could actually be a turning point, and the best thing that could have ever happened to you. To give an example of this in terms of relationships: at one point, someone might perceive the start of a romantic relationship as the best thing that has ever happened to them. Later on, the relationship might turn sour and the couple might choose to separate. At the point of separation, the start of the relationship might change its meaning and now be perceived as the worst thing that has ever happened. The meaning of events might change with time. So, do not give a setback more weight than it deserves. This could be the event that pulls you toward a better destination. You have the power to define the meaning and the result of everything that is happening around you. That's how powerful you are.

Some people declare defeat at any minor inconvenience and carry that misery forever. They tend to operate from a closed or a fixed mindset and have a hard time looking past their self-imposed limitations. Others lean in, look for the lessons, listen to the nudges of the universe, and flow with the redirection that moves them faster toward their vision, and in many cases takes them farther than they could have ever imagined. People with a winning mindset know that there are plenty of opportunities and that this is not the end. They move with internal self-confidence and determination to make this happen; determined to define their story with success.

Looking under the surface and questioning the wisdom that comes with a setback is essential for learning the lesson and stopping the same cycle from repeating—the joys of OBSERVE! As difficult as it is to admit, pain is often the catalyst for rapid growth, transformation, and for setting you on the path that you were actually meant for.

What might be perceived as a setback presents an opportunity to reevaluate how you operate and reflect in a way that you wouldn't have considered if everything was running on autopilot. Is this the best strategy? Or what strategy provides a better return? Are you in the right market? Or is it time to pivot? Is this the best use of your time and resources? Could you be doing something else with a bigger impact? What course of action will help move you closer to your vision with less resistance?

Some say setbacks are stepping stones; others call them slingshots that launch you forward. The reality is, setbacks are whatever you decide they are, they are whatever you want them to be. What matters is how you respond, and how you rebuild momentum. There is a famous quote attributed to Swiss psychiatrist Carl Jung, that expresses the idea that no tree can reach Heaven, unless its roots reach down to Hell. This is not to say that you need a breakdown to thrive. What is required, though, is what we have been referring to in this book: awareness of what is actually happening, perseverance, and a personal operating system—a set of practices that support your entrepreneurial resilience.

When you started your business, you might have had a clear plan that made sense in your head, and on paper. This might be referred to as a business plan. Business plans are a good exercise for self-reassurance; they help us sleep better at night knowing we have some sense of what this venture will look like and what *could* happen. Reality proves that nothing is certain until we actually go through the experience and get the results. This is confirmed by the fact that almost all business plans fail and results often end up nowhere near what we expected.

The Ebb and Flow of Business and the Roadmap to Winning

What's interesting is that the longer you're in business, the more you understand the ebb and flow. You graduate from being a dreamer to becoming someone who truly understands what it means to be in business and navigate uncertainty. And, if you're resilient enough to stay true to your vision, your confidence will expand because deep down, you'll know you can handle whatever comes your way; you'll experiment, learn, adjust, and see the fruits of your labor. There is a tremendous sense of self accomplishment that results when you figure out that your business, the system you have built, is actually working: it's providing value and generating income.

However, there is an ebb and flow in business. This is what seasoned founders understand and many fragile beginners miss. Building a winning legacy depends on how we navigate change and the more challenging seasons that no one sees, it's in rolling with the punches. It's in the decisions we make when everything's uncertain, when the pressure is high, when the results aren't showing yet. That's where our character gets built and our future is shaped.

Winning isn't just about achieving an outcome; it's about staying true to ourselves through the process. Winning is a decision we make in our mind first before seeing results materialize. Winning is not waiting for certainty before taking action, it is in having faith and choosing to be on the path most rewarding to you, even though it can feel like you are walking this path alone, and others around you are not on board and cannot understand what it is you are trying to do. Winning comes in this choice, the choice to keep walking through the lonely season.

Winning comes from having radical self-belief and knowing that we will get to the other side, that no matter what the existing circumstances are, whatever the current battle is, we are capable of pulling it off and are determined to remain resilient. The old saying "the only constant is change" is true. Difficulties are not permanent and will pass. It is important to work with what we have, do the best we can, and keep learning and pivoting until further notice. With the ever-evolving nature of business, this holds true despite whichever level of business we are in.

A question on your mind right now might be: "how do I know the right next step? What is the right action to take as I navigate the mess I am in?" Well, thank you for asking. Here is a reliable process you can follow that allows you to lean on your intuition and find the best possible course of action:

- **Step one.: control the inputs.** Filter out all the noise and distractions. Set clear boundaries around your time and attention, so you can remove outside distractions that do not serve.

- **Step two: introduce meaningful perspective.**
  Reach out to your support system: your consultants, coaches, mentors, or people who have navigated similar experiences. The goal here is not to outsource decision making, but to form a clear perspective.

- **Step three: take an intentional break.** We covered three types of breaks in the previous chapter (mental, emotional, and structural); a simple uninterrupted walk might do the trick at times. The purpose here is to clear your mind and process what is happening before taking action.

- **Step four: lead from a winning identity.** Envision your winning self, the most capable, grounded, and successful version of you, further down the road. How does this person think, feel, and act? From that vantage point, what decision would they make in this situation?

In many cases you will find that this future version of you, the winning version that is operating from a broader perspective and is looking at this situation, would respond differently than the way you were initially tempted to respond. Questioning the mindset and actions that this future self takes allows you to gain perspective on what really matters at this moment, make better choices, and get better results. That's the main difference between your current self and your ridiculously successful future self, the way they think and act. The quicker you embody your ridiculously successful future self-identity in your day-to-day decisions, the faster you get there!

If you picked up this book, and it resonated in any way, shape, or form, the probability that you are wearing multiple hats in your business is high. You might as well start the day putting your winner hat on, assume that role as well and carry that spirit, the return on this simple act is incredible.

Sure, different founders start from different points on this journey. Some come across more resources than others; some have more connections, etc. But with the right approach, none of these matters. When you see that the journey can take all sorts of turns, you realize that the starting point doesn't matter and should not be a reason to walk around defeated.

You can start over again at any point with whatever resources you have: financial, human connections, knowledge, etc. What matters is being true to your vision, knowing that *you are capable* of pulling it off, and doing your part: setting yourself up for success, building the capacity to increase your entrepreneurial resilience, and leading from grounded roots.

What you might not typically hear from other "successful" founders that attempt to portray confidence at all times is that everyone is experimenting until they find out what works. People generally do not prefer to talk about their hard times, setbacks, and failures as it hurts the ego, or because they do not want to deal with the judgement. The reality is that no one for certain holds all the right answers outright or has everything figured out. Imposter syndrome never disappears, despite previous success. It shows up every time we experience something new, as our brain perceives what is not familiar as a threat. With time we just become more confident experimenting, as we accumulate evidence from previous experiences that we will be fine.

A common challenge for us builders, visionaries, and founders is that our ideas evolve and we keep moving our goalpost. It is easy to get consumed by chasing the next chapter and forgetting how far we've come.

A few years ago, you might have dreamed and prayed to have a business, to be in the place you are today. And here you are, at that milestone, yet consumed in your day-to-day demands, worried about the future, and the next goal ahead. Before anything else, you owe it to yourself to take a deep breath and celebrate this and every moment. I have covered this previously but it is very important, so I will say it again: if you haven't booked that vacation yet, and you feel it is time, here is another sign to do so!

Every comeback story in business follows a similar pattern. It starts with radical acceptance, owning the reality without shame. Then comes a moment of recommitment or realignment, where we strip back what no longer fits and reconnect with what's true. And, finally, we emerge with a more honest vision, a way of operating that's grounded in depth and deeper knowing, not ego. At least that's the case when we've actually attempted to learn the lessons.

As ridiculous as it sounds, and as much as I hated living in stress for those few years, looking back I'm thankful for what happened. It is difficult, if not impossible, to be thankful in the moment as you are trying to figure your way out of a challenging situation. You're worried and unsure about what will happen next, and you're trying to talk to God but He does not seem to be getting back to you. However, making it through to the other side provides perspective and that's when things start to make sense.

I've never been in a pressure cooker, but the experience strikes me as being similar to what it must feel like: you go through radical change you didn't know was necessary. My vision has always been big, and there was no way it would be realized if I kept doing what I was doing. My strategy, the service niche I was in, and the market were not best suited for where I wanted to be. My business breakdown led to a re-evaluation, a recognition of that truth, and a redirection.

Show Up Every Day

That season allowed me to realize that resilience doesn't look like powering through at all costs, simply because powering through at all costs was not working! It looks like pausing, reassessing, returning to what matters, and pivoting as required. Sometimes all you have to do to be successful and see things through is to just show up every day, even when you do not have the answers you seek.

The beauty of the journey is that it eventually filters out the static, the people who only show up when you're winning, and the distractions that once pulled you off course. You see clearly what is serving your purpose and what is not.

Through all of this, it is important to let go of any feeling of resentment, as holding on to it only holds us back. We need to forgive any previous injustice we experienced. Most importantly, it is important to forgive ourselves for any setback or missteps along the way. Forgiving ourselves might prove to be more difficult than forgiving others. Remembering that we are human helps, so keep you head held high and keep moving with purpose.

Dwelling in the past is what keeps many stuck. They can't seem to move past previous setbacks. The key to moving forward is developing confidence, knowing that despite what happened, you have what it takes and are capable of making the end destination better.

This journey will keep evolving, and so will we. If we follow the stories of the best CEOs, we see a common theme of continuous learning, doing a lot of reading, embracing a preferred way of leading (i.e., a personal operating system) and a focus on constant evolution. These all help give founders their edge.

Staying in this game for the long term—and amplifying your business results—begins with a choice. It's the choice to step into a new version of you before the results show up. That choice invites aligned action, and aligned action shapes outcomes.

The Resilient in Business OS™ isn't just a framework; it's a personal operating system for founders who want to fully live life on their terms and lead their businesses effectively, like a boss. It keeps you steady as things shift, grounded in what matters, and aligned with your values as you build. It gives you the tools, structure, and support to create a legacy that lasts, even in the chaos that business inevitably brings.

Life's too short to keep playing small, stay stuck in survival, or hold everything together alone, and never fully stepping into what's possible. True success and freedom are available for everyone who chooses it. Your vision deserves the right structure, one that allows you to be more resilient so you can see it through.[5]

---

[5] To learn more, or take the next step visit www.resilientinbusiness.com

ACKNOWLEDGMENTS

Thank you to my parents for all of the help and support you have provided me through the years. I realized long time ago that paying you back will not be a linear equation, so *thank you*.

Thank you to both my sisters for being here on the journey.

Thank you to my uncle, Hassan Younes, for the support that is always present and shows up with no questions asked. You have saved the day over and over again, more than you are aware.

Thank you to my friends, the ones who genuinely showed up when they did not have to: Igor Konović and Zaid Al Qaysi.

Thank you to my team, the people who showed up, were supportive, and remained committed when things were messy.

Thank you to Susan Crossman from Crossman Communications for helping edit this book and for pushing back where necessary, until we reached this amazing outcome.

Thank you to the great professionals who were generous enough to say a few nice words about this project in the praise section.

The final thank you goes to God, for everything.

Free On-demand Workshop
Resilient in Business

A guided experience to pause, reflect, and explore what the ideas in this book reveal about your current reality as a founder or CEO.

Includes a brief walkthrough video led by the author.

resilientinbusiness.com/resources

www.ingramcontent.com/pod-product-compliance
Lightning Source LLC
Chambersburg PA
CBHW051634120626
46551CB00014B/2078